P9-DGJ-688

The President and
the Public Philosophy

MILLER CENTER SERIES ON THE AMERICAN PRESIDENCY

The President and
the Public Philosophy

KENNETH W. THOMPSON

LIBRARY
BRYAN COLLEGE
DAYTON, TENN. 37321

LOUISIANA STATE UNIVERSITY PRESS
Baton Rouge and London

82153

Copyright © 1981 by Louisiana State University Press
All rights reserved
Manufactured in the United States of America

DESIGN: Joanna Hill
TYPEFACE: Linotype Baskerville
TYPESETTER: Service Typesetters

LIBRARY OF CONGRESS CATALOGING IN PUBLICATION DATA
Thompson, Kenneth W.   1921–
The President and the public philosophy.
(Miller Center series on the American Presidency)
Includes bibliographical references.
1. Political science—United States. 2. Pres-
idents—United States. I. Title. II. Series:
White Burkett Miller Center. Miller Center series
on the American Presidency.
JA84.U5T48   353.03'1   80-26165
ISBN 0-8071-0795-6

TO RANDOLPH P. COMPTON

Contents

IV THE FUTURE AND THE PRESIDENCY

The President and
the Public Philosophy

Introduction

The writer who sets out in search of a public philosophy may aspire, as Walter Lippmann did, to build a contemporary theory of natural law. His goal may be the definition of certain enduring and universal principles for the governance of nations everywhere. Another approach is one that seeks to discover perspectives on politics and public affairs that for a given era help in the definition of problems and policies and is widely accepted by different political groups banding together in broad-based political coalitions. This latter approach seeks to determine public attitudes and public moods; it makes use of the findings of public-opinion surveys. A third approach may appropriate the insights and findings of the former two and may even imagine it can bring about their synthesis. Its goal is a living political philosophy for a particular time and place, though the principles it evolves may have relevance beyond limited historical circumstances.

What is common to all three approaches is a resolve to introduce coherence into the pattern of endless incoherence that constitutes the political process. As one political scientist writes: "In all that furious motion of campaigns, lobbying, and lawmaking, and in the vast and confusing output of statutes, policies, and programs issuing from it, one can discern certain ideas at work."[1] Without a formulation that gives some minimum coherence of purpose to public endeavors, broader social interests are overridden by a surge of special interests.

No responsible student of American government would claim that a public philosophy would eliminate the clash of special in-

1

terests. Historically, conflicts have often increased when individuals or groups have proclaimed a more general viewpoint. Countervailing philosophies have emerged in response to a controlling philosophy. Bourgeois theories have been offered as alternatives to feudal theories. Socialist philosophies have taken their place alongside the doctrines of nineteenth century liberalism. Hitler's precepts of National Socialism, however blatant, crude, and brutalizing, rested on notions of German romanticism whose authors sought to counter the failures of German liberals to grapple with the problem of power. Whatever the function of political ideas, it is illusory to believe that a public philosophy could do away with political competition or the struggle for power. Conservatism breeds liberalism and liberalism Marxism; public philosophies taken seriously may in fact increase political conflicts.

Nonetheless, political rivalries which fail to transcend stark conflict between combatants who confront one another "red in tooth and claw" and whose political lives are merely "poor, nasty, brutish and short" are from a moral standpoint an absurdity. Politics divorced from purpose descends to the level of political street-fighting. It ignores the single truth that every enduring humane Western political philosophy has accepted, namely, the essential duality of human nature. Regnant political theories have rejected "the model of conflict which some observers see in contemporary societies in which warring groups, emptied of any vision of the social whole and guided only by the residuum of their private concerns, quarrel over the spoils."[2] Those who defend the truth of the duality of human nature argue that it is as false to deny man's goodness as it is to ignore his bestiality; as wrong to speak only of his rationality as to overemphasize his irrationality; as erroneous to point to his boundless sympathy as to neglect his cruelty; as misleading to stress good intentions as to pass over destructive consequences; as one-sided to praise man's virtue as to forget the biblical reminder: "The good that I would I do not: but the evil which I would not, that I do." At the core of man's nature, good and evil coexist in what is fundamentally and persistently an ambiguous relation. Any public philosophy must take account of the human condition.

The political consequences of man's predicament in being at the same time selfless yet selfish and virtuous yet corrupted are expressed in a classic American view of governance attuned to the dualism of human nature. The founding fathers observed that if men were devils, government would be impossible; if men were gods, government would not be necessary. Because man's nature curiously blended good and evil, a form of government was required to hold evil in check and to channel man's virtue. Thus the aims of government and of the social order were to craft and tailor political institutions to suit the requirements of the human condition.

Within this tradition, the Federalist Papers remain the best textbook in democratic political theory. The founders recognized that Americans were the inheritors of two thousand years of experience in the relation of politics and the nature of man. For this tradition, democracy was not the transcending of politics but the wise application of certain timeless political principles. The Federalists were more cautious about man's absolute virtue than were political idealists. The founders never doubted that Americans as a society of free people were in pursuit of the good society, but they spent less time in proclaiming it, more time in seeking ways and means for achieving it. Even if one acknowledges, with the historian Charles A. Beard, that the Constitution represented the work of a certain economic class, it remains a document which kept open the channels of opinion and political participation for everyone.

The course that this inquiry will follow is one of testing out the prospects for a public philosophy in an utterly different world from that of the founding fathers. In the era of the founders, it was possible to think both of a strong national government (Alexander Hamilton) and a political order leaving room for individualism and political participation at the local level (Thomas Jefferson). Government was viewed as an instrument for confronting the challenges inherent in a new industrial order while preserving the strengths of rural life. Less explicit were the principles for helping the disadvantaged and underprivileged, establishing America's place in the world or controlling the damage resulting from dislocations occurring anywhere within an interdependent system. The founders, to a man, were generalists rather than specialists; they called up the aura of the Renaissance man. They embraced a set of values which comprised a common body of political ideals.

Writing of the 1960s and 1970s, Harvard professor Samuel H. Beer can say: "We do not enjoy a public philosophy. But there is such a thing as equilibrium without purpose. The balance of social forces today tends toward a kind of peace."[3] The question is whether "equilibrium without purpose" and a political armistice is the closest approximation to a public philosophy for the 1980s and what remains of the twentieth century. Inextricably linked with the pursuit of a new public philosophy is the role we assign to the presidency, the most powerful executive office in the world. It is not by accident that past discussions of public philosophy have been linked with elaborate accounts of particular presidencies, in particular those of George Washington, Thomas Jefferson, Abraham Lincoln, Theodore Roosevelt, Woodrow Wilson, Franklin D. Roosevelt, Kennedy-Johnson and, joined by differences, Nixon and Carter. It is the president who sets the tone, helps shape moods and expectations, and provides or fails to provide a framework for public understanding. The main excuse for a book on the president and the public philosophy is the empirical fact that public philosophy and executive vision, historically and in the present, are bound together.

To say that is not to discount the tides of history and deep-flowing social forces which surround and control political events in each successive human epoch. For example, the widely read and broadly educated men of culture to whom the founders turned for political wisdom have in our time been supplanted by technocrats and professionals, of whom Everett C. Hughes has written: "Professionals profess. They profess to know better than others the nature of certain matters, and to know better than their clients what ails them or their affairs." Physicians consider that they are best qualified to weigh costs and benefits and organize health delivery systems requisite for good medical care. Social workers demand the right to prepare social legislation. "Every profession considers itself the proper body to set the terms in which some aspect of society, life, or nature is to be thought of, or even the details, of public policy concerning it."[4] Moreover, what is true of professions is true with a vengeance of special-interest and single-issue groups and of ethnic politics as they seek to dominate the political realm. So far-reaching and all-pervasive are the claims of specialist politics that they leave little room for statesmanship or political wisdom as envisaged and described by the founders. From the 1950s, government and public service has drawn on "professional specialisms" with an effect sometimes described as the "technocratic takeover." Democratic politics has displayed two contradictory trends: the diminishing participation of the citizens with devotion to the common good and the vastly intensified participation by those who voice the noisy claims of special interests.

Another change with far-reaching consequences for a public philosophy is the loss of public trust in institutions and ideals, legislation and leaders. Every year, more people ask if cities, states, and the nation are ungovernable. The fact that an American president in the summer of 1979 would dare to speak, without fearing the political consequences, of a national malaise demonstrates how deep are public concerns. Earlier in the 1970s, a former vice president questioned whether Americans could find answers to any of the most grievous problems. At the grassroots, the preoccupation of ordinary people has apparently shifted from long hours devoted to clarifying public issues to narrowly private and sometimes narcissistic concerns.

The other level at which a public philosophy seems remote from practical attainment by Americans but is urgently needed is in relation to the world revolution that has undermined America's credibility and its confidence in itself. In the 1940s, leaders warned of a world revolution generated by international communism. That revolution in the form that was prophesied has never come about despite Soviet penetration into far-off places like Afghanistan. Another kind of major transformation has taken place, however, as the United States discovered it was no longer self-sufficient or economically the most productive or most successful in world markets, or even necessarily the military and moral leader in a changing international order. As important as this transformation itself are the reactions of Americans. One response to America's declining fortunes has been to look for scapegoats, to protest that heedless and unpatriotic leaders too little concerned with arms buildups or trade expansion have dragged down America. The United States had been number one; from a chauvinist perspective, any decline can only reveal a failure of leadership. That this rather narrow, egocentric view should have prevailed and become dominant in American political debates merely highlights the need for a public philosophy.

Yet the requirements of a contemporary political philosophy are formidable. It is easier to look back to an earlier political tradition than to fashion a new one for an unfathomable future. It is possible to locate a ground of common belief which has supported the American political tradition and, however imperfectly recent presidents may have defined it, this tradition has given the Republic inner strength and the ability to hold tensions and conflicts within manageable limits. The question is whether the nation will be able to rally this body of belief for building a new public philosophy. Since changes such as our society is experiencing can rend a civilization asunder, our efforts for a public philosophy must involve the recovery of lasting principles of politics while we consider some of the root causes of the crisis of confidence in the twentieth century: the threats to human survival, the decline of public and private trust, and the perplexing relationship between internationalism and nationalism in the present era.

I The Root Causes
of America's Crisis
of Confidence

1

Survival Imperiled:
The Threat of Illusion
and Despair

A cloud of uncertainty and self-doubt hovers over anyone who undertakes to discuss the great public issues of the day. Lines which have long divided ebullient liberals and wary conservatives have broken down. Noted historians who once called for strong executive leadership now warn of the "imperial presidency." Philosophers who in the 1950s and 1960s had viewed public servants as a collective version of the Good Samaritan complain of thousands of young bureaucrats issuing millions of rules and regulations and applying them without judgment or discretion. The pervasive power of the mass media, having promised an educational revolution transforming mankind, has instead brought encapsulated versions of the day's events into everyone's living room often generating more heat than light. The trivialization of public life is a clear and present danger promoted by a curious admixture of the media's drive for high ratings and the self-serving practitioner of government leaks.

Old hands in Washington look back with a certain nostalgia to that ancient stereotype of the stodgy and self-conscious aide clutching purported secrets to his bosom. A vast outpouring of "show and tell" manuscripts prepared by Watergate personalities in and out of jail has spread doubt and distrust; the government memorandum to be circulated among a handful of colleagues is shared with the kind of apprehension foreign service officers displayed during the era of Senator Joseph McCarthy. Public leaders no longer trust their confidences to immediate associates and it is decent, hard-working Americans, not strident spokesmen of the

9

far right or far left, who suffer, thus bringing into question the capacity of government to rule and of businessmen honorably to manage the economy. Our wisest thinkers ask, "What of mankind's survival in an increasingly insecure world?"

The profoundest, most lethal threat to any civilization, Arnold J. Toynbee discovered, arises from within, however endangered a people may be from barbarians outside their boundaries. Inflation and distrust, single-issue special-interest groups and a growing profusion of intractable problems resisting solutions have begun to erode the cement of shared goals and purposes that have held the American community together. Twenty-five years ago it was the parsons, the philosophers, and a few historians who warned of a "time of troubles." Today a similar note is being struck in corporate board rooms, in union hiring halls, and in the nightly commentaries of the pundits. Friendly travelers to other lands discover that "the American problem," now worldwide in scope, has become all too familiar east and west and north and south. Peoples who once had hope are being strangled by despair.

ROOT CAUSES OF THE PROBLEM

If societies around the world have grown dispirited and face the future without answers to grave and unsettling problems, the first question to raise is how are we to diagnose the root causes of such problems. For nearly two decades I worked alongside three dozen or more biomedical and agricultural scientists who approached the task of improving the world's health and of fighting world hunger in what to me was a novel spirit. At first glance, I was distressed that they appeared, if not callous and indifferent, less concerned than I about pressing and immediate crises, problems, and catastrophies. Floods and famines, earthquakes and epidemics were not their responsibility, I was told. Their numbers were too small and their knowledge too fragmentary to join the world's fire fighters. I remember my shock when biological scientists expressed skepticism about an American president's call for a multi-billion-dollar crusade to eradicate cancer or when agricultural scientists showed lack of enthusiasm for huge shipments of grain to rescue starving peoples. Their argument was that the scientist's first duty was to look for root causes, not symptoms. His task was to lay the scientific foundations on which others might build the delivery systems to serve hundreds, even millions of people. As months passed, my sense of moral revulsion diminished and grudgingly I came to respect their single-minded concentration. In the public arena, I heard less and less about dollars doing away with cancer or shipments of tons of grain ending famine in India. By comparison, my Rockefeller Foundation colleagues took me to maps on which they had plotted the few remaining pockets of malaria, primarily in Ethiopia, or had marked out the countries achieving self-sufficiency in rice or wheat through use of the new varieties and fertilizers which were keys to the Green Revolution. When I asked the secret of their success their answer was invariably the same: seek out the root causes and concentrate on what is primary not secondary.

With the passage of time, my admiration and respect for these success stories in health and food production was mixed with a certain envy. My colleagues' task was clearcut and direct whereas mine in assisting university development in newly independent states was complex and many sided, with educational development interconnected with every other facet of the culture. It was not that problems of food or nutrition were wholly unrelated to culture. That a connection was unmistakably present could be seen in the texture of the rice preferred by the people in Indonesian culture compared with that in Philippine culture. Yet adapting new varieties to cultural preferences through plant breeding was a manageable undertaking and the so-called miracle rice (IR-8) was transformed into hundreds of local varieties through agricultural experimentation in laboratories in the Philippines and throughout Asia. By comparison, the one effective laboratory for university development was the society at large; educational systems to meet human need had to be integrated with cultural realities in each society. Higher education, which had been a perpetuator of culture in Europe and America, tended to be a destroyer of traditional culture in Asia and Africa. Food production was directed to a universal primary human need but education ramified out, touching every facet of the social and political system.

The lesson social scientists learned working side by side with medical and biological scientists in the developing countries was that the first step in seeking the root cause of a problem was facing up to the problem. For the humane scientist to deny that war or group conflict was a perennial problem because he found its effects distressing or uncivilized would be as incongruous as for the biological scientist to set aside the need to recognize, diagnose, and treat a particularly virulent disease which by its manifestations was debilitating to suffering peoples and offensive to the healthy observer. Yet to the early modernizers or to self-confident nation builders, tribalism in Africa appeared to be little more than a temporary obstacle or impediment to early westernization, democratization, or development. Their state of mind did not lead them to search for root causes. It might be comforting for Westerners to be able to point out to the most rabid African nationalist that England, France, and Germany had set aside ancient nationalist rivalries and had joined together to form a European community. However, if nationalism remained the most powerful social force in Africa, the Westerner who spoke endlessly to Africans about ridding their minds of nationalism was unlikely to be called on to offer advice and counsel. The same could be said of tendencies to overlook persistent non-Western religious forces in a country such as Iran, which could not be comprehended by drawing analogies with Western religion.

As I reflected on the unmistakable differences in approaches by the humane and the biological scientists and the contrast between the biological and the social orders, I became persuaded that human illusions are inescapably a dimension of social reality and stand in the way of the search for root causes. At one level, all science is a unity, all human endeavors are purposeful. Even for the most rigorous scientist, response to a felt need or social purpose is the first step toward scientific progress. Thus the need for improved health led historically to the creation of the medical sciences just as the need for roads and bridges led to the science of engineering. It is said that urgent social and human problems are a greater spur to scientific advance than a thousand universities. Problems and needs precede scientific inquiry and, in the words of

Kant, sound reason approaches nature "not in the character of a pupil, who listens to all that his master chooses to tell him, but in that of a judge, who compels the witness to reply to those questions which he himself thinks fit to propose." In this one respect, the political and the natural scientist stand on common ground. All science begins with a question.

However, at precisely this point, differences become more important than commonality. The biological scientist may possess the same emotions toward the eradication of cancer that the political scientist does toward the elimination of war. However, for the scientist at work in his laboratory, emotions are irrelevant to and separable from his investigation, since in the physical world facts exist independently of what anyone may think of them. For the social investigator, facts may be changed by the desire that they be changed, for their existence is never wholly independent of an observer's attitudes or of the attitudes of those he seeks to influence. Indeed the purpose of the social observer is itself one of the facts, inasmuch as every political or social judgment tends to modify or rearrange the facts on which that judgment is based. Thus the aim of most present-day observers of capitalism—including many socialists—is the defense and preservation of capitalism. Whereas Marx maintained he was the founder of a new science and Marxism owes much of its driving force to its scientific pretensions, his approach to the analysis of capitalism was inseparably linked to his goal of destroying capitalism. The same was true of the late Professor Kinsey who brought to his research on sex an all-consuming purpose of changing legislation on sexual behavior. Those who point to a vital social need or the necessity of solving a problem unquestionably perform a valuable function. They run the risk, however, of the utopian scientists whom Engels criticized for believing that "socialism is the expression of absolute truth, reason and justice and needs only to be discovered in order to conquer all the world." The risk is resting content with answers that are predetermined by the questions asked.

The search for the root cause of social problems is further complicated by the impulse in the social observer to not only describe reality but change it. Within modern democratic societies the movement of political and social scientists in and out of government has become a permanent part of the political landscape, prompting the British historian Herbert Butterfield to write: "Whenever I learn of another political scientist having moved into Whitehall or the White House, I feel a headache coming on." Evidently Butterfield's indictment is directed less against political scientists than against the tendency of men of thought to suffer shipwreck when they undertake to become men of action. Reinhold Niebuhr pointed to a related problem when he wrote: "If the democratic nations fail, their failure must be partly attributed to the faulty strategy of idealists who have too many illusions when they face realists who have too little conscience."

Yet we have it on authority of the greatest Western playwright that "dreams are the stuff life is made of." Mankind has been propelled forward by bold visions and grand obsessions that were folly to those who opposed them. The rub comes when illusions breed disillusionment. How are we to distinguish between visions that carry men forward and those that lead to disillusionment? During my work with a technical assistance agency, I felt dismay on hearing an agricultural colleague announce that he and his associates were capable of turning a country's agricultural production around. I found in these words a distressing air of pretentiousness. The saving grace for my colleagues was the state of the agricultural sciences whereby the means could be made available for the attainment of outrageously ambitious goals. Not only were the techniques and tools at hand but the resources for financing them were abundant in the West (a consortium of donor agencies provides hundreds of millions of dollars of assistance to international agricultural research centers around the world). The gulf between the proud boasts that a handful of outsiders could transform an entire agricultural system and the reality of peasant cultures stubbornly resistant to change was not as great as I had assumed.

On the other hand, thoughtful observers have singled out illusions in which public expectations have far exceeded political reality. The first illusion concerns the role of executive or presidential leadership. In America, we are living with what my colleague James S. Young has called the troubled presidency. Young has observed: "Once seen as a solution to problems, the centralization of power in the White House has come to be seen as a source of problems in society." Ever since the public disillusionment with executive power in the face of Lyndon B. Johnson's abdiction and Richard M. Nixon's overthrow, the "ritual destruction of the President" goes on from administration to administration. The presidency has become the lightning rod for all society's discontents. On the other hand, even friendly critics note a certain insufficiency in presidential capacity: too many unrealized and unrealizable public expectations; changes in the political process involving the decline of political parties and the phenomenon of television campaigning; the resurgence of congressional staffs; a sense of public boredom with presidential initiatives, and widespread unease that the institutionalized presidency has grown larger than is necessary or even manageable. The illusion of the imperial presidency has something to do with the disillusionment which has swept over public thinking on the presidency leading Professor Young to call for "retrenching Presidential power in order to preserve it . . . winding down Presidential government in order to save the Presidency for the things only it can do . . . disregarding much of the rule-book written in the 1950s and 1960s that shows the President how to get power . . . disengaging the Presidency from many of the problems that public expectations, campaign exigencies, news media pressures and the Washington establishment will demand that the President do something about . . . getting the Presidency substantially out of the business of managing the executive branch: ceding large parts of that domain to Congress, courts and cabinets, but not ceding the President's power to preempt or intervene when reasons of state require . . . and regaining the ability, within the Presidency at least, to distinguish between true and pseudo-crises, real alarms and false ones, threats to the Republic and mere problems for the administration."[1] In summary, it means statecraft based more on a strategy of presidential self-restraint, less on a strategy of an all-powerful and everywhere visible presidency.

A second illusion concerns the public's trust in its leaders and institutions in the public and private sector. More than two decades have passed since Walter Lippmann warned that democracies ran the risk of politicizing and making public the private lives of political leaders and privatizing their public responsibilities—the latter, as one outspoken cabinet official in the 1950s was to say, because "what is good for General Motors is good for the country." Ours has become an era of exposé. The people's appetite for being told that their leaders have feet of clay is apparently insatiable. Coupled with the public's thirst for the inside story, the national pastime of cutting leaders and policies down to size has left us devoid of heroes and perhaps of heroic policies. Spokesmen of the media tell of receiving a flood of often half-substantiated or unsubstantiated reports thrown up from within public or private bureaucracies. On the side of the media, investigative reporting which lies somewhere between yellow journalism and responsible analysis of great public issues has moved toward the pinnacle of contemporary journalism. Those waging campaigns within bureaucracies to add to or subtract from the stature of political or business leaders or defend or oppose policies through leaks are also the reigning bureaucrats whose rules and regulations are laid down as standards for public and private conduct across an ever widening spectrum of society. If the fourth estate has strayed outside the boundaries of responsible journalism, self-interested allies within the bureaucracy have added fuel to a movement which began with the worthy goal of educating the citizenry but has ended with a "whodunit" story. Is it any wonder that confusion has multiplied and trust has diminished in the public at large?

The third illusion is related to the second. It involves the moral and political dilemma of the media. We are engaged, says the most respected of network news anchormen, Walter Cronkite, in the trivialization of public life. News encapsulated in thirty- to sixty-second fragments is hardly designed to educate the uninformed or to place an important story in context. Gone are the commentaries of Edward R. Murrow, Elmer Davis, or Eric Sevareid; the hard-pressed public, however eager to make sense of complexity, receives pitifully little guidance from analysis by well-informed observers. Communication which was touted as a medium for universal education has become a channel for freeze-dried news.

With the emergence of special-interest groups, the political process itself has contributed to another illusion. American and Western societies have been held together historically by a vision of common interests. The rise of narrow single-issue groups, controlling, it is said, up to 3 percent of the vote in crucial elections and comprising the swing vote nationally and locally, has transformed American politics. The decline of political parties has speeded this trend. The legacy of the late 1960s has emphasized the rights and influence of special interests whose concerns had been neglected for generations: minorities, ethnic groups, and the underprivileged. It would be an exaggeration to claim that such interests had ever been fully reflected in historic definitions of the public interest. Their rights ultimately deserve to be integrated into new formulations of national purpose. What threatens any definition of national unity is the assumption that the Republic is nothing more than a congeries of special interests owing no allegiance to any definable notion of the common good. In the 1950s, Winston Churchill warned fellow members of the Conservative opposition: we are party men defending party interests but above all we are defenders of the national interest. The national interest was the primary interest, he concluded, even for party men.

A fifth illusion which has preoccupied Americans and, I presume, Europeans has been a belief in the easy harmony of interests and of *the right solution* to every practical problem. Today every developed country is plagued by apparently insoluable problems for which no simple agreed remedy is at hand. Inflation no doubt is the most troublesome of all such problems and national consensus is lacking on its resolution. In the absence of consensus, national groups have reverted to a Hobbesian answer to economic problems: a war of each against all. Lacking confidence that agreed upon common solutions could ever be reached, each economic group, seeking its own ends, has freed itself to gouge every other group. It may well have been illusory to suppose that what was good for labor was good for management or vice versa. Too many solutions have been pursued that ignored the tangible loss which one group's gain involved for all other groups.

The final illusion is one fraught with the most fatal consequences for all. Not one civilization but all mankind stands on the brink of mutual destruction in conflicts in which all are involved. World community and world government, which intellectual leaders proposed as the surest guarantee of world peace in the 1940s, are apparently beyond the reach of existing sovereign states. In the absence of a dependable worldwide security system, each nation has pursued its security through the accumulation of national power. One nation's security has become another's insecurity; nations are caught up in what has been called the security-power dilemma. Collective security which in the 1940s and 1950s had been viewed as an effective approach to peace has broken down and, according to a former secretary of state, nothing has been put in its place. Once more the gap between a noble illusion and present-day political realities has come to threaten survival, in this instance of all mankind.

IMPERILED BY DESPAIR

If illusions beyond reach are a threat to human survival, despair also endangers mankind. Modern man, having lived with recurrent crises, has also learned to cope with a vast array of difficulties. Societies new to international conflicts have demonstrated unexpected resiliency and an ability to contain localized disputes. Yet the threat of mutual annihilation persists, and an all-pervasive anxiety hangs over every policy decision. The shattering of cherished illusions and the absence of viable alternatives has left public leaders bereft of faith and troubled by doubt. Anxiety, which is a generalized form of fear and guilt over policies that appear to have failed, has overcome strong men and led to social malaise. Initiatives sometimes undertaken precipitously have added to self-doubt and magnified the sense of uncertainty. Despair has fallen over the citadels of power and, *a fortiori*, over those standing outside and offering criticism from the safe vantage point of freedom from responsibility.

The road back to renewed faith in leaders, institutions, and policies demands, first, that men and nations free themselves from the sense of powerlessness that has swept over leaders and followers alike. It is puzzling to account for the degree and extent of our unease. Because all the great choices appear to require collective action, the solitary individual resigns himself to the belief that because nothing works, nothing is possible, and therefore nothing matters. Public apathy and personal withdrawal are the result. Even courageous leaders declare that human problems have outrun human resources and they can but lament that within a society in which all the once promising approaches to public issues have failed, no one has responsibility for the general welfare. What follows is a cycle of individual doubt, indecision, and vacillation by political leaders and harsh judgment by popular critics—all reinforcing and feeding on one another. Doubting itself, society despairs of finding the way out of a tragically self-confirming process.

The suspicion persists, however, even when the diagnosis of despair points to major sources of malaise and unrest, that something more fundamental is involved. Child psychologists tell us that young people who have experienced little or no success fall into behavior patterns in which they apparently choose to fail or are unable or unwilling to engage latent energies in a quest for success. Yet history teaches that civilizations' noblest triumphs have come from those who persevered without the comforting illusion of omnipotence. Washington had no illusion that the thirteen colonies were all-powerful or Churchill that the British in the defense of freedom possessed overwhelming military strength. Could it be that today's leaders who earlier exaggerated national power or the uniqueness of America's national purpose have not yet learned to live in a world where power is being redistributed? Are Western nations, as appears to be true of their chief executives, destined to pass through an era of retrenchment before they set out once again in pursuit of bold new national and international goals? Are those who predict that the 1980s will be a period of consolidation world-wide likely to be the best prophets? When and how will national leaders who enunciate national and international purposes inspire renewed confidence and escape the criticism that stirring words in the 1970s evoke only boredom in the public?

It may be that Andrew Jackson's advice to his troops "to elevate them sights a little lower" would be helpful in public policy. There is a moral duty for a nation, as for a family, to establish priorities and bring its commitments and capacities into balance. Americans, like the Europeans in another era, may have to learn to live in a world in which their absolute monopoly of atomic power and world leadership has been relatively short-lived. Yet the challenge may be greater and the rewards more enduring for Americans in regional and international cooperation than in the will-of-the-wisp illusion which an influential American publisher, Henry Luce, named "the American Century."

Paradoxically, the "time of troubles" for Americans and Europeans could provide a breathing space for relearning forgotten lessons of politics and statecraft. One lesson may be that successful postwar foreign policies have not only rested on towering moral visions but on practical forms of international cooperation based on a convergence of national interests, the Marshall Plan being the classic example. Another lesson is that the founders of the American Republic, at least in their more reflective moments, never assumed that good public policy would mirror exclusively the interests of a single region, class, or group. Because they were widely read and profoundly educated in the political classics, leaders such as Jefferson, Madison, and Washington understood the ancient tradition of moral reasoning which taught that political choice rested on a balancing of competing goods. In his memorable work *The Moral Decision*, the brilliant American legal philosopher Edmund Cahn argued that moral choices are made not between right and wrong, but between two rights which cluster, compete, and sometimes conflict with one another. In the American constitutional system, the right to a fair trial competes with the right of the public to know through freedom of information. The Supreme Court has declared that freedom of speech does not give the individual a right to cry fire in a crowded theater. Human rights around the world as a goal of American foreign policy must be balanced against the goal of normalization of relations with

China and the Soviet Union and that of maintaining secure allies in the Cold War. The quest for new friends in foreign relations must be balanced against the continuation of old and trustworthy alliances. Peace must be preserved through adequate arms and national power to create a stable balance of power while nations simultaneously attempt to turn down the spiraling arms race. Leaders must seek to build a world based on universal international relationships, always remembering that we live in a pluralist society of politically and culturally independent states. Within nation-states, they must balance competing interests and claims, none of which can be ignored but no one of which can be fully satisfied. The political consequences of moral reasoning introduce both new possibilities and inescapable limitations about which leaders must speak to the public, as John F. Kennedy did when he observed that President Lincoln was often a sad man because he learned that in politics no one can have everything he wants.

Despair would be less pervasive if we accepted the inevitability of tragedy. Politics for nations and individuals is suffused with both triumph and tragedy, but in recent years we have heard far more from our leaders of the former than the latter. Illusions would be less crippling and despair less far-reaching if leaders spoke more thoughtfully of the tragic element and less boastfully of vaunted victories and triumphs. The political and diplomatic process has more than its share of inescapable gains and losses. It is instructive to remember the wise counsel of George F. Kennan, who has warned that diplomatists who claim a victory in negotiations have destroyed thereby the prospects of continuing the diplomatic process and the necessary give and take. The political vulnerability of the negotiators of almost every sovereign state is such that following any diplomatic encounter they cannot return to their publics acknowledging defeat. What is true of diplomacy is likewise true of national politics. Each side must have its gains as well as its losses, evidence of successes as well as inevitable compromises to bring back to its public. It is noteworthy that the Carter administration achieved its most conspicuous foreign policy success through what Churchill would have called diplomacy conducted in all its privacy and solemnity at Camp David, with a minimum of press releases and ill-timed or ill-considered off-the-cuff public pronouncements of dramatic successes by one or the other of the parties. The ordinary citizen has only to ask himself what kind of resolution would be possible for deep-running disputes within the family, the school, or the church if every limited and provisional sign of progress or fallback were tallied up on a public scoresheet for pundits to praise or condemn. The illusion that public diplomacy pursued uncritically is the road to peace is another contemporary illusion which has haunted present-day negotiators.

It may also be true that world leadership in our time is more likely achieved through the force of moral example than by bold presidential proclamations. Unhappily, the full weight of the American example is consistently obscured by strident and contentious debates which have become part of the ongoing political process. Minorities long neglected and overlooked in American society have achieved opportunities that a few brief years ago appeared permanently denied them. While the debate goes on and steps toward group fulfillment and advancement are being pursued even in an era of retrenchment, the most vocal civil rights leaders acknowledge privately that substantial progress has been realized. Despite the alarms and doomsday pronouncements incessantly voiced about the dire state of the American economy, scores of large foreign investors transfer their funds to the United States. The number of new jobs has multiplied, totalling three million in 1978, and underrepresented segments of the American population—women and blacks—are annually joining the labor force in a period of widening social and economic opportunity without precedent in American history. Equal opportunity in education has advanced beyond the point the skeptics and disadvantaged dreamed possible with new programs at community colleges, work-study, and on-the-job-training. Whatever an observer's political persuasion, it is indisputable that a vast array of political and economic innovations, let alone far-reaching new scientific research, has been carried forward in the 1970s. The first important initiatives have been taken in conserving energy, stabilizing the dollar, and funding local and national human resources programs without jeopardizing investment and growth in the economy. Although the adversary nature of the political process may conceal the tides of history working for good, future historians almost surely will point to profound social advance in the 1960s and 1970s. Crime rates dropped during the 1970s at least in certain sec⌐rs and key groups among the disinherited and disadvantaged have begun to take responsibility for their own destiny. America began to draw some credit for having been in the vanguard of the movement for national self-determination, for some one hundred new nations have become active participants in international society. In summary, American society is on the move far more dramatically and powerfully than the casual observer of national or international affairs, lacking a sense of history and a balanced perspective, comprehends or appreciates.

If this is true, why the all-pervasive despair? What is the cause of our malaise? Why the national mood and the protracted "winter of discontent"? I have suggested that national attitudes reflect deep-running tides or forces at work which have both rational and irrational components. Towering illusions and grand obsessions, when they are the sole guides of the ship of state, may carry societies toward a new channel course but may also leave them grounded on jagged shoals. No seasoned captain would dare to bring his ship into port taking his bearings exclusively by the stars. He cannot afford to ignore local waters. It remains painfully true that American politics has as often been damaged by noble idealists as by cynical realists. Ends must be brought into balance with means, purposes with capacities, vision with prudence. Disillusionment and despair tend to follow illusions that have failed or appear to have failed, and history records a cyclical movement in politics: reform followed by retrenchment and by reform again. The amelioration of despair in time of consolidation depends on keeping hope alive to prepare the way for a new era.

The ultimate test, of course, is how nations respond to the challenge of adversity. Having said that a nation's example is the most powerful and important expression of its values, one must point to another vital factor. What may be lacking in the United States and perhaps in all countries today is a public philosophy. Paradoxically, such a philosophy was more nearly at hand in the founding days of the Republic when concern for political ideas of lasting value reached new heights. Two elements were essential then and are indispensable now for such a philosophy: first, certain bedrock principles subject to continuous reexamination concerning the nature of man, of politics, of society and the nation-state, including its relationship with other nations; and second, concepts of public interest and the common good which transcend parochial interests. An American senator has recently proclaimed that more fundamental than any public philosophy is a philosophy of the private sector and he has proposed shouting from the housetops that America alone among states is "the party of freedom." Significantly, the debate over individual freedom and the debate over states' rights and national interest was one that was subsumed within a broader discussion of the public interest by men such as Jefferson and Madison. It would be tragic if Western thought should settle for two philosophies—one public and the other private, one national and one local or particular—when such interests were inextricably joined especially within and among interdependent societies. Undergirding them both and at a deeper level must be fundamental philosophical principles that have universal meaning and application. The principles of a public philosophy must be addressed to man's nature—neither wholly good nor irreparably evil but capable both of profound goodwill and harsh and demonic cruelty. They must deal with man's noblest ends and his narrowest self-interest. Such principles must speak both to individual and collective interests, balancing them in diverse ways to meet specific needs and discovering some wider framework for ordering the two. They must deal with the rational and irrational in man's nature without assuming categorically that one has taken the place of the other for all time simply because men are better educated, more prosperous, or shielded from the harsh threats of nature.

No one can say from whence such a public philosophy will come or, if it should be produced, who will embrace it. Earlier efforts, including some in our own day by our most respected leaders and thinkers, have been unsuccessful and abortive. The absence of a widely accepted and viable public philosophy suggests the

awesome magnitude of the task. What can be affirmed and staunchly defended is that without a public philosophy, every advance or
retreat, success or failure by any public or private leader will be
challenged and disputed; it will be interpreted outside the unifying
framework and the context that alone can give it meaning. We
shall have no basis for judging great public efforts or worthy private enterprise if we lack a conception of man and society and of
where society should be tending in the late twentieth century. Instead, all of us, and not least professional observers, will be reduced
to hasty judgments, partisan political opinion, and oversimplified
evaluations which interpret public affairs from the too narrow
calculus of personal victories or defeats. The grandeur of a dialogue about the common purpose of civilized men fashioned
through wisdom and sacrifice over the centuries will disappear
from public discourse. The pressures of noble goals in tension
with practical necessity will be lost, and politics will lack its timeless expositors and clarifying voices. We are in deep trouble today
because no one seems capable of helping us to see our problems in
their broader historical and philosophical context.

The journalist Meg Greenfield, writing about the American
debate over SALT and the language in which the issues had been
posed, warned that complex technical jargon has taken the place of
straightforward political argument. The heart of the issue, she
maintains, is political, not scientific: "How each side can protect its
arsenal in a way that will deter the other from attack or even from
pushing and shoving, and in a way that is . . . mutually reassur-
ing." She adds: "Science is an important calculation here. But
politics—the character and intentions and weaknesses and strengths
of the affected people and institutions—is profoundly what it is all
about. . . . One of the things worth demanding of our politicians
this year is that they discuss this vital range of questions in compre-
hensible and relevant terms."[2] And comprehension depends on the
understanding which comes from ordering a succession of political
debates within some broader political and philosophical framework, our single most urgent survival task.

If the problem has been defined and the root causes diagnosed
with some measure of clarity, where are we to turn for help?

Scholarship has become too specialized, political speech writing too clever by half, and politics too fragmented and divisive. The nation's boldest thinkers and most eminent teachers of a quarter century ago, whether theologians, columnists, or political philosophers, who once offered guidance, have passed from the scene. Prestigious establishment commissions on national goals have left scant trace of their well funded labors. The tempo of public life and mass communications is not conducive to political philosophy. Crises follow one another in rapid succession, and the best that society can offer may be the art of muddling through, thanks to leaders who are successful problem-solvers and self-acknowledged pragmatists. If we conclude society is too frustrated by circumstances and too impoverished intellectually to fashion a more enduring response, we had better say so and be prepared to pay the price.

In the 1950s, the board of trustees of a leading private foundation renowned for its work in health and agriculture around the world announced a modest program of grants in legal and political philosophy. This worthwhile effort to stimulate political thought was short-lived; more urgent survival problems crowded out concern with the public philosophy. However, this initiative lent dignity and encouragement to the work of a handful of younger thinkers, some of whom continue to make important long-term contributions. It is conceivable that other initiatives can be found more appropriate to the times as counter-forces to society's preoccupation with its immediate, most pressing, and urgent problems. For history teaches that those leaders who have helped men and women understand present dangers and challenges in the past— the birth and survival of a young and fragile republic, its preservation in the face of bitter civil warfare, its recovery from a devastating depression, and its safe passage through two world wars— have done so by lifting men's minds to higher levels of political understanding. They have extracted from present necessities certain enduring political truths; they have seen the general in the particular. If their successors are to free men from despair and substitute credible ideals for paralyzing illusions, they must do so by following similar routes and highways. Without such efforts, wisdom, as T. S. Eliot warned, will be lost in knowledge and knowledge in information. The ultimate irony would be the failure of Americans to explain American society, its values and its politics, its institutions and its economy, just at the moment its major rival, the Soviet Union, was losing most of its moral and political authority in Europe and the world.

The questions raised in a more comprehensive analysis of a public philosophy for the future are the subject of Part II of this book. Taken together, they are the core of the work. In Chapter 4, I intend to focus on the concept, the organization, and the public philosophy of the presidency. I hope to consider the relevance for the remainder of the twentieth century of the bedrock principles and basic concepts delineated above. But first, I propose to examine in greater depth two root causes of the current crisis of confidence, namely, the decline of public and private trust and the complexities in the relationship between internationalism and nationalism.

2

The Decline of Public
and Private Trust

The idea of trust has been throughout history a cardinal tenet of religion, politics, and human relations. In biblical religion, the prophets called on man to place ultimate trust in God saying: "Thus saith the Lord; Cursed be the man that trusteth in man and maketh flesh his arm, and what heart departeth from the Lord. . . . Blessed is the man that trusteth in the Lord. . . . The heart is deceitful above all things and desperately wicked: who can know it?" (Jeremiah 17:5–9) In Reinhold Niebuhr's words: "The basis of trust [in the Christian religion] is not in any of the constructs of human genius or any of the achievements of human diligence which arise periodically to imposing heights and tempt men to put their trust in their own virtues and ability."[1] Christian trust resides in God and God's laws, not in man's ability to fulfill those laws. Yet such is man's pride that he places his trust in false gods: material abundance, human progress, his nation or culture or church or class or in the perfectibility of human reason. Optimism about man's nature was for Niebuhr more dangerous than human despair because few men are willing to accept permanent despair. Instead they build little worlds of meaning and trust around themselves carved out from a fragment of the cosmos. In the midst of chaos and confusion, men seek hope in self-sufficiency buttressed by optimistic creeds of progress, salvation through a political leader, or social class or faith in some social utopia.

Man's faith and trust in the fragmentary communities of existence has characterized societies since the earliest chapters of human

28

history. Primitive man placed his trust in the tribe or the nation in order to propitiate the gods. The complexity of such trust, however, was illustrated in the Judaic concept of the chosen people. The tribe or nation legitimized its claim on man's ultimate loyalty by maintaining that God had chosen it to realize his purposes on earth. Yahweh's relation to the Hebrew people as a chosen race was illustrative of faith in other primitive cultures. The tribe or the nation, whatever its accomplishments, required a link with some transcendent being. Even the most optimistic creeds that worship some attribute of human nature hedge against man's failures by seeking reference points outside human history. Breakdowns and catastrophe in a nation's history were so commonplace that trust depended on something more permanent than national destiny or political success. As Niebuhr describes it, "The Hebrew prophetic movement found a source of the meaning of human existence which not only transcended any possible chaos in history but actually predicted catastrophe as the inevitable consequence of man's sin against life and God."[2] Religion for the prophets was more than a compensation for failure and defeat. Nations as men are mortal. To trust the virtue of collective man is therefore as false as to trust wicked and deceitful individual man. Religion establishes a source of trust outside the chaos and destruction of human societies.

This source of meaning and of ultimate trust has been undermined or compromised by a succession of historical events. The faith of early Christianity was apocalyptic, awaiting the second coming of Christ. When this vision was disappointed, a devolution of the source of trust occurred as Christianity made its peace with the secular and political world. It became "a new cement for social cohesion in the Roman Empire." It served temporarily to give coherence to a political system that had by then begun to decay. Faith in God intermingled and became corrupted by faith in Rome and in the citizen of Rome. St. Augustine sought to rescue Christianity from this union with an empire facing destruction. He offered Christians an interpretation of their faith based on a City of God which was eternal in contrast to an earthly city doomed by "self-love in contempt of God." Whether in victory or defeat, the earthly city was corrupted by man's self-love and trust in himself. But Christianity would survive the fall of Rome because its home was the heavenly city.

Ironically, however, Augustine contributed to a further decline in religious faith and trust. In part his writings were an answer to Roman pagans who charged Christianity with weakening faith in the empire, thereby causing its collapse. The decline of the Roman Empire was due, he argued, not to the rise of Christianity but because of the consequences of man's fall. Regardless of the shape of human institutions, the reality of finite man refusing to concede his finiteness would lead to society's decay: "It is vain that men look for beatitude on earth or in human nature." Every man as he strives for power shows himself willing to inflict injury and loss on other men. It is true that man was given power over every living creature but he has corrupted as he sought to dominate other men. Rome sought not wealth and comfort but pursued "nobler" goals such as glory, honor, and fame. Trusting to themselves, Romans came to rule the whole civilized world. However, the glory of conquest and subjugation of non-Romans by force carried a fateful price. Glory and honor were civilizing objectives because their attainment required society's homage and respect. However, for Rome the desire for glory was overwhelmed by the desire for naked power. In Augustine's words, "He who is a despiser of glory, but is greedy of domination, exceeds the beasts in the vices of cruelty and luxuriousness."[3]

For Augustine, then, fallen men cannot achieve perfect trust; in every community from the family to the empire, suspicions and quarrels intrude. Even within the family—for man his most intimate community—treachery and deceit replace trust. Friendships are flawed by man's selfishness and his failure to perceive and respect the hopes and fears of others. Even self-knowledge is marred by the ruling passions. Peace is at best a "doubtful interlude between conflicts."[4]

The further decline in trust resulted paradoxically enough from Augustine's vision of the City of God. He set that city against man's earthly city; the rule of the former was "love of God in contempt of oneself" but of the latter "self-love in contempt of God."

A small minority of mankind has been chosen to receive eternal salvation. These men constitute the City of God and after the day of judgment they will live forever in perfect peace in the presence of God. Meanwhile, the human part of this city is a single society spread throughout the world: "This heavenly city, then, while it sojourns on earth, calls citizens out of all nations, and gathers together a society of pilgrims of all languages, not scrupling about diversities in the manners, laws, and institutions whereby earthly peace is secured and maintained, but recognizing that, however various these are, they all tend to one and the same end of earthly peace."[5] The visible church is more closely related to the Eternal City than any other human institution but its members include both the reprobate and the elect. At one point, Augustine appears to say that its boundaries are not coterminous with the Heavenly City. The faithful are pilgrims or sojourners in this life who long for the end of history and the time when they join the Eternal City. Others were to contend that Augustine confused the two cities.

For Protestant theologians such as Niebuhr, Augustine erred by identifying the heavenly city with the church. This error led Augustine to place too much trust in man, in this instance the redeemed man of the church. Even redeemed man who lives by grace remains finite, sinful, and subject to historical aberrations of his own generation and the ambitions and pride of special groups and classes. The church remains a human institution dependent on those classes in society who can most easily support it and who benefit from those injustices that serve it and the church. In Niebuhr's view: "Augustine, in short, was responsible for the great heresy of Roman Catholicism, the heresy of identifying the church with the Kingdom of God and of making unqualified claims of divinity for this human, historical and relative institution."[6]

Medieval civilization expressed both the strengths and the weaknesses of Augustine's theology. Trust in God came to mean trust in the church and the noblest attainments of medieval Europe arose out of its religious foundations. Papal leaders of the moral stature of Gregory VII and Innocent III left a legacy of faith that inspired civilization's noble achievements. Yet as temporal rulers the popes fell prey to the pretensions of all rulers. "Wherever religion is mixed with power and wherever the religious man achieves power, whether inside or outside the church, he is in danger of claiming divine sanction for the very human and frequently sinful actions, which he takes and must take."[7] Cursed be the man, Niebuhr concluded, paraphrasing Jeremiah, who places his trust in the earthly church. Christians in medieval history overlooked the peril of mixing too uncritically their trust in God and trust in man.

Protestantism was born in rebellion against the Catholic heresy. It struggled to free itself from the pretensions of believing that man could achieve the Kingdom of God by saintliness and virtue. The Protestant reformer trusts the grace of God while distrusting the goodness of man. Yet Protestantism falls victim to another temptation. It places its trust in the pious man. Protestantism rests its faith not in Christian civilization but in the pious individual who, interpreting the Scriptures without intermediaries, is capable of knowing God's will. If only other men were as pious as the individual Christian, God's Kingdom would come to the world. Niebuhr asks, what have been the historical consequences of Protestant individualism? He responds:

> Sometimes Protestant piety has degenerated into barren orthodoxy; sometimes into Puritan self-righteousness. . . . Sometimes the very relative moral code of lower middle-class life . . . [becomes] the sign and the proof of a "God-fearing man" in Calvinistic Protestantism. Sometimes the ethics of money-getting is sanctified in the same manner. On occasion the pious Protestant is as certain that his civilization (capitalism) is God's particular civilization as the Catholic was certain of feudalism.[8]

Niebuhr proclaimed with the prophets a judgment on Protestantism, which he found wanting as all other religions: "Cursed be the man that trusteth in man," even when he is pious man, or perhaps, especially when he is pious man.

THE IDEA OF TRUST IN POLITICS

If religious thinkers have questioned the possibility of placing one's trust in man, the literature of practical politics abounds with skeptical references to trust. A French proverb from an anonymous source reads: "God save me from him I trust." In a passage dated May 26, 1783, Boswell's *Life of Samuel Johnson* records the following: "I would rather trust my money to a man who has no hands . . . than to a man of the most honest principles." An Italian proverb reads: "Trust was a good man, but Trust-not was a better." A Yugoslav proverb warns: "Trust only yourself and your own horse." An English proverb of the fifteenth century proclaims: "In trust is treason." Thomas Fuller, writing in 1732 in *Gnomologia*: "If we are bound to forgive an enemy we are not bound to trust him." Shakespeare echoes in *Henry V*, Part Two, a similar view: "Trust none; For oaths are straws, men's faiths are watercakes."

If political writers and politicians have placed limits on the possibility of trust, they have sought to redefine its role in more specific and pragmatic terms. The nineteenth-century Italian nationalist Count Camillo di Cavour is quoted as having counseled political leaders: "The man who trusts other men will make fewer mistakes than he who distrusts them." For Niccolò Machiavelli in his advice to the prince, the appearance of trust was essential for success in politics. Trust in politics, however, was subject to constraints, for as Machiavelli wrote:

> How laudable it is for a prince to keep good faith and live with integrity, and not with astuteness, everyone knows. Still the experience of our time shows those princes to have done great things who have had little regard for good faith, and have ultimately overcome those who have made loyalty their foundation. . . . Therefore a prudent ruler ought not to keep faith when by so doing it would be against his interest, and when the reasons which made him bind himself no longer exist. If men were all good, this precept would not be a good one; but as they are bad, and would not observe faith with you, so you are not bound to keep faith with them.[9]

The disputations among the interpreters of Machiavelli have centered upon passages such as these, some arguing that cynicism dominated his views, others insisting that his intention was merely to warn against the danger of weak governments that were too virtuous to have recourse to power. A similar dispute surrounds the oft-quoted remark of the British ambassador Sir Henry Wooton, who defined an ambassador as "an honest man who is sent to lie abroad for the good of his country." It was said that Sir Henry scribbled this remark as a joke in an album at Augsburg. His plea that he had written in jest did not suffice to convince his monarch, James I, that he should continue in diplomatic service. Yet the image of the diplomat as an honorable spy persisted. Diplomatists of the sixteenth and seventeenth centuries provided grounds for the suspicion that they left aside private morality when they entered public service. In Sir Harold Nicolson's words: "They bribed courtiers; they stimulated and financed rebellions; they encouraged opposition parties; they intervened in the most subversive ways in the internal affairs of the countries to which they were accredited; they lied, they spied, they stole." Yet Nicolson, looking for the permanent qualities requisite for the good diplomatist in every age, put truthfulness first alongside intelligence and character. Acknowledging that "the worst kind of diplomatists are missionaries, fanatics and lawyers; the best kind are the reasonable and human skeptics," Nicolson modified Wooton's statement by adding: The diplomat must return to negotiate another day.[10] His reputation for credit and confidence in the long run will prove more lasting than his momentary success through deception. For the negotiator should recollect that he is likely for the rest of his life to be judged by whether men are ready to trust his word. Trust is in this regard the cement of diplomacy, the nexus of negotiations if the diplomat is to return to negotiate another day.

What is true of diplomacy is true of politics. Lying is not, in the long run, good politics either with your friends or enemies. A student of the political machine in Chicago of the late Richard Daley—perhaps the most successful political machine in the history of American politics—has asserted that Daley and his immediate associates almost never lied. Successful politicians will not promise to do anything unless they can deliver it. They are wiser not to say anything. In this respect, it is possible that politicians in Chicago are no different from politicians in Peking or Moscow or elsewhere in the world. A precinct captain will not promise a constituent he will do something unless he can get it done. A ward committeeman will not promise a job to a precinct captain unless he can deliver it. Mayor Daley did not make promises unless he was confident he could back them up. Politicians of this school operate on the principle that it is better not to lie to your friends because, if you lie, they will never trust you again. In the same way, it is also better not to lie to your enemies because that too is dangerous. For political reasons, they need to be able to rely on your word. Therefore, while people may lie in politics, practice shows it is not good politics.

At the same time, politics and diplomacy offer countless examples of selective truth telling. It is not only politicians and diplomatists who find it prudent to extract some parts of the truth and omit others. Family life suffers when a mature and experienced father takes as his guide with his children the maxim to tell the truth, the whole truth, and nothing but the truth. Selective truth telling may be an essential requirement for bringing young people to maturity. The strong father may wish not to throw all his burdens and professional and business problems on his family. An internationally known scholar has observed: "I do not expect the president of my university to tell the worst things about the university." Referring to public servants, another observer has noted that saying "honesty is the best policy" is one of the most immoral statements that has ever been made. It implies that the only reason for honesty is that the civil servant has been paid for his honesty and that his capacity for judgment has no intrinsic moral base. On August 3, 1914, German Chancellor Von Bethman-Hollweg declared that the treaty guaranteeing the neutrality of Belgium was "a scrap of paper." His statement was accurate, objectively, but it was a politically stupid declaration. The chancellor's values as an honest man clashed with his interest to conceal what Germany was doing.

As the crises of international politics increase, the pressures on ethics become greater. As concern for national survival grows more urgent, the pressures to violate what are recognized in personal life as moral principles multiply and increase. In the Second World

War, a radical shift occurred in attitudes on morality. The historians of the Franco-Prussian War of 1870 in Prussia and France respectively had described, on one side, the widespread popular indignation against the guerrilla actions of the French and, on the other side, the military actions of the Germans against the French. In World War II, the legal and moral distinctions between civilian and military personnel were obliterated both for Axis and Allied powers. The technology of warfare was in part responsible for the change but so was a general decay in respect for human life stimulated by technology.

The attitudes in international society with respect to killing resemble lawlessness on the frontier. In modern civilized communities, men do not carry guns for self-protection as they move about in society. However, that need existed for long periods of history when the moral constraints against killing were hedged about by the requirements of survival. The condemnation of killing in present-day civilized nations has become virtually an absolute prohibition. Once society loses its ability to protect its citizens and self-defense replaces an effective system of law and order, however, the moral rules against killing are bound to change. In short, circumstances affect the relevance and application of absolute moral principles. What is true of killing is true to a still greater extent of lying and therefore of the context in which trust can be preserved in politics and diplomacy. The normative function of a moral code remains intact but its compulsive force, the actual normative force of that code, is qualified by the situation. Something more than slavish conformity to an absolute moral code is essential to trust, for such conformity is unlikely even in the best of worlds.

THE IDEA OF TRUST IN HUMAN RELATIONS

The problem of trust in human relations confronts difficulties not too dissimilar from those in religion and politics. A host of far-reaching social changes have compounded the problem. For one thing, morality and trust involve primary relations between two persons, yet modern-day society has become increasingly a society based on secondary relations. Trust depends to an important degree on face-to-face relations, but, with the kaleidoscopic movement of peoples and groups across a broad social and geographic spectrum, such relations are becoming less and less possible. I may dislike my neighbor but neighborliness gives me the chance to know him as I cannot know a stranger. My children's life-style may offend me but, given compassion and cultural empathy, I have a chance of understanding the reasons of their folkways. In my childhood, I learned some of the causes for the ancient maxim: never trust a stranger. Much as it offended my youthful liberal outlook, the disruptions of family life in a small midwestern town by strangers who called on my father, a clergyman, to rescue them from human predicaments that were beyond salvation led me to qualify my early view. Today we are, as sociologists remind us, a nation of strangers. The nation's mobility has scattered families over three thousand miles of expanse. Trust all too often must be taken on faith. Personal relations are ever more complex because of the transitory character of most human contacts.

The weakening of the hold a common religion once had on people further complicates the basis of trust. The society operates on many value systems, not a single unified and widely accepted system of religious and moral beliefs. We are a pluralist society of many religions, some of which are more threatening to other religious systems than no religion at all. Catholics and non-Catholics, Christian Scientists and non-Christian Scientists, charismatic Christians and noncharismatic Christians, the Moral Majority and its critics are as likely to be arrayed against one another as are Christians and non-Christians. Young people question the foundations of those religions that stand in the way of their unfolding life-styles. Religion which once was a source of unity threatens to become a profoundly divisive force as liberal Jews oppose orthodox Catholics on urgent social issues like abortion.

We are also a divided people on the issue of business and government. The business ethic is rooted in values such as profits and production; the public ethic speaks of welfare and helping the poor. The one ethic tends to be tough-minded, growth-oriented, and committed to freedom; the other calls for planning to meet human needs and new social problems and is reconciled to controls. The former looks finally to the bottom line of profits and losses; the latter calls on society to recognize neglected human problems. Given the wide gulf that separates business and government, the call for understanding and trust too often falls on deaf ears.

Society is also divided morally and intellectually along major social and group lines that make trust more difficult to achieve. Periodically, we call on the people to trust this dominant intellectual or political movement or that representative social group. Trust science, we say, and the fruits of scientific achievements span our common life from medical advances to placing man on the moon. Yet the most scientific nation in Europe initiated World War II and the West's scientific prowess has led to the building of weapons that threaten all mankind. Trust reason and education, others proclaim, and trust mass communication. Yet as Reinhold Niebuhr argued: "The ubiquity of the written word, which, in the opinion of Condorcet, would bring salvation to the world, can spread vulgarity and prejudice as quickly or more quickly than it can spread enlightenment." Trust intelligence, yet "intelligence merely raises all the potencies of life, both good and evil." Trust intelligence joined with piety, says liberal Protestantism, yet such a marriage, as with projects of the 1930s advanced by the champions of the social gospel, may lead to an enervated sentimentality. For "piety may rob the intelligent man of his critical vigour and intelligence may destroy the indispensable naïveté of all robust religion."[11]

"Trust youth" was the rallying cry during and after America's ordeal in the world wars and the Vietnam War. Old men perpetuate wars and accept ancient evils. Old men are tired, timid, and cowardly about change. Youth is heroic and self-sacrificing, capable of giving the world a fresh start. Youth brings fresh conscience to man's problems and, spurred by moral outrage, uproots civilization's gravest evils. Yet youth [lacking a sense of history] is also impatient and prideful. Youth provides the most fanatical disciples for the culture's most hysterical political and religious movements. Others say trust the rich who are not tempted by need. Yet from "robber barons" at the turn of the century to corporate leaders offering payoffs for new economic opportunities abroad, the rich have not distinguished themselves for their absolute incorruptibility. Trust the poor, social reformers urge, for the poor have little and deserve much. Yet the poor man who gains power becomes as untrustworthy as the rich. The reasons are those cited by Niebuhr, who more consistently served the poor in his ministry than any other twentieth-century theologian:

> If the poor man is generally trusted . . . he will achieve the power to overturn society and build a new social order. He will then cease to be the poor man and become the powerful man. The prophets who led him in the wilderness will become the priest kings of the new order. The new social order may be immeasurably better than the old one but it will not be free of the temptation to corrupt and to misuse power.[12]

Surely this has been true of the Marxist paradise of the poor, the Soviet Union. The prophet who has gained power will kill his fellow prophets as Stalin did Kamenev and Zinoviev or exile them as he did Trotsky. Too unqualified a faith in the poor man— labor, the proletariat, or the disadvantaged—will generate an equilibrium of forces making the poor man untrustworthy.

Trust in human relations depends on something broader and more fundamental than calling forward one movement or group to be the bearer of trust. Every movement and every group has its strengths and its weaknesses. Each has its contribution to make. But in Niebuhr's critical view "there is no form of human goodness which cannot and will not be corrupted, particularly in the day of its success. Let the wise man destroy the superstitions of the present; and the poor man disprove the pride of the wise man; but then a new prophet must arise to convict the priest king of the poor of the perennial sins of mankind to which he is also subject."[13]

THE PRESENT CRISIS OF TRUST

Whatever the historical sources of trust, present-day America faces a new crisis of confidence and trust. At one level, the historic problems are manifest in the unfolding of nationwide mistrust which has weakened the nation's confidence in itself and in successive presidents. John F. Kennedy spoke of trusting a new generation of leaders who had taken up the torch from those who had led the nation in World War II and the aftermath of that great struggle. Yet even before the young president was struck down, youth showed itself unable to resolve the nation's problems. Youth did not free the president from the blunder of an abortive invasion of Cuba in the Bay of Pigs nor an ill-fated confrontation with Premier Khrushchev in Vienna. Lyndon B. Johnson innaugurated more social legislation than any president in modern times but fell victim to the struggle in Vietnam which more prudent national leaders had described as "too tough a nut to crack." President Nixon's rallying cry was trust "Middle America," but his administration was corrupted by its willingness to violate the law in its campaign against those who opposed its political objectives. President Carter proclaimed his determination to trust the people, but the tension between his populist tendencies and the necessities of governance proved a fateful stumbling block to his presidential leadership.

It would appear that public and private trust, if it can be restored at all, must depend on something more than the rather sentimental, inconsistent, and unrealistic approaches of recent leaders. The first step toward mutual trust is a bold recognition of the limits of trust. If America has become a nation of strangers representing a diversity of interests, cultures, and languages, then communication and understanding have become more difficult. Interpersonal relations, which are more impersonal in an ever more complex world, may for the foreseeable future rest on the most tenuous foundations. Trust that presupposes the absolute goodness of man is romantic optimism, and romanticism throughout human history has been transmuted into cynicism and disillusionment. Confidence in the goodness of life cannot rest on confidence in the goodness of man. Deep human trust means discerning the goodness of creation beneath all the corruptions of human nature.

Trust, in short, depends, for religious thinkers most of all, on a recognition that evil cannot overwhelm the good. A man's tranquillity results from the knowledge that the evil which others show toward him is not very different from the evil he shows toward others, that the trust others betray calls to mind the trust to which he himself does violence. Belief that man is incapable of perfect trust should not lead to withdrawal, supernaturalism, or otherworldliness. The answer to trust in others can never be found in removing oneself from others. Nor is cynicism an answer, for cynics judge others for falling short of their ideals but justify themselves for achieving norms they themselves construct. From a religious standpoint: "The best antidote for the bitterness of a disillusioned trust in man is disillusionment in the self. This is the disillusionment of true repentance."[14]

Trust for political men depends on greater realism about the political ties that bind men together. "Interests never lie" was a political axiom that Winston Churchill periodically invoked quoting his ancestor Lord Marlborough. At one level, trust rests on what Churchill described as the one helpful guide in politics, honor. In international politics, honor leads a nation to keep its word and to act in accordance with its treaty obligations. Yet honor is a concept of political ethics, not of higher morality; for, as Churchill wrote: "It is baffling to reflect that what men call honour does not correspond always to Christian ethics. . . . An exaggerated code of honour leading to the performance of utterly vain and unreasonable deeds should not be defended, however fine it might look." The same Churchill drew together a grand coalition to thwart the expansion of Nazi Germany, maintaining that, as had been true for four hundred years, it was the common interest of the states of Europe "to oppose the strongest, most aggressive, most dominating Power on the continent and particularly to prevent the low countries falling into the hands of such a power." Churchill reasoned from common interest in concluding: "Therefore, it seems to me that the old conditions present themselves again, and that our national salvation depends upon our gathering once again all the forces of Europe to contain, to restrain, and if necessary to frustrate, German domination."[15] With the rise of Hitler, Churchill said bluntly he would make a pact with the devil himself to contain Germany's expansion and, shortly thereafter, Britain gave assistance to the Red Army's struggle to hold back the Nazi juggernaut. On negotiating with the Russians, the prime minister, whom the Russians had charged with trying to strangle Bolshevism at birth, prophesied that the Soviets could be counted on to keep their agreements provided they were in the Russian national interest.

For politics, therefore, trust is dependent on the interests of a statesman, a party, or a nation. Once common interests are identified, for example in the avoidance of nuclear war, men and nations will keep their word, even across a deep ideological divide. Religion and politics come together in their evaluation of trust in that neither depends wholly on the virtue and goodness of other men. Paradoxically, nations recognize that agreements are most needed, as with strategic arms limitations, precisely when trust is lacking. If trust is to be sustained, interests once identified must be adjusted, preserved, and maintained. What is therefore required is continuing political and diplomatic contact and exchange with one another. The good and decent man who keeps his word may reestablish trust and confidence. This task is one of utmost urgency for the people, the nation, and the presidency.

3

The Duality of the
International System:
Internationalism and Nationalism

The twentieth century has been heralded as the era of internationalism, a century when the common purposes of mankind have
more and more replaced narrow national interests. From the
heroic words of President Woodrow Wilson to Barbara Ward's
inspiring concept of spaceship earth, the tides of history seem to
be moving irresistibly toward the emergence of one world. Successive revolutions in science and technology have shattered the
limitations of space. Man, who for millennia was confined to his
tribe or neighborhood, has broken through boundaries of locality,
state, and nation. The United States of America, which for two
centuries had been a union of contiguous states, has burst the
bounds of a single, integrated national territory. Alaska and Hawaii
have become the forty-ninth and fiftieth states not because they are
geographically part of a single land mass but because modern aircraft have transformed physical remoteness into territorial proxim-
ity. It takes less time for today's traveler to reach Honolulu from
Los Angeles than the horsedrawn traveler required to make the
trip from Philadelphia to New York in the days of the founders.
The revolution in transportation has enabled the nation as a
whole to draw closer to people on the outposts of American territory than was possible for citizens of contiguous states in an earlier
period. Presidential candidates campaign more easily in Hawaii
than their predecessors at the turn of the century did in Cali-
fornia or Florida. If villages, towns and states within the nation
have been bound together by mid-twentieth-century forms of

transportation, farflung nation-states have been welded together by transcontinental and intercontinental airline schedules.

If transportation has revolutionized space, the earth has been knit together by a worldwide system of communications. No location on the surface of the earth or on distant planets is too remote for instantaneous telecommunication. The average American citizen follows American and Soviet astronauts in space; a walk on the moon is viewed in the living rooms of millions of ordinary Americans. The president's travels in India and Africa are as vividly displayed and graphically reported as are his week-long journey on the *Delta Queen* down the Mississippi. The secretary of state's shuttle diplomacy in the Middle East has the same immediacy for the mass media as the coming and going in Washington of the Russian ambassador to the White House or the Department of State. Messages and pictures are beamed from satellites to virtually every point on the globe. From a technical standpoint, no country is too distant, no conference table too remote for the commentator's voice or the television cameraman's know-how. Because of the drama of international diplomacy or the excitement of Olympic competition, the far-off event has become more commonplace for some Americans than political or social happenings within local communities.

The revolution in warfare wrought both by national attitudes and by science and technology has altered the shape of the world. In the case of global warfare, it is difficult to find much that is positive or constructive in the far-reaching shift in world conflict. In the words of Arnold J. Toynbee: "Evils which hitherto have been merely disgraceful and grievous have now become intolerable and lethal."[1] Modern wars resemble most the "wars of religion" of the sixteenth and seventeenth centuries; they are marked by a fanaticism which unites the fervor of religion with the grim business of war. Quincy Wright described such wars in his monumental history, saying: "During this period wars, while not unrelated to political or even economic interests, were ostensibly fought for religion."[2] Fanaticism was evoked against an enemy who was not only a military foe but also a moral and political miscreant. The play of political and military forces as they intervened in the religious competition of the era intensified the ferocity of warfare and conflict. Particularly in Germany, France, England, and the Low Countries, this relationship was decisive in determining the religious beliefs of the people and in aggravating the struggle for power. Each sectarian faction sought a shortcut for the attainment of its religious mission through the use of military force. The French-Huguenot Wars of 1562–1594, the Dutch Wars of Independence of 1568–1648, the Thirty Years' War of 1618–1648, Queen Elizabeth's wars against Ireland, Scotland, and Spain, and Charles V's wars in Mexico, Turkey, Peru, and France all partook of a religious character. Of these conflicts, the historian Jacob Burckhardt wrote:

> Of all struggles, the most appalling are the "wars of religions," more especially those . . . in which a religion has taken on a strong national coloring and a people is defending itself in its religion. Among civilized peoples they are the most terrible of all. The means of offence and defence are unlimited, ordinary morality is suspended in the name of the "higher purpose," negotiation and mediation are abhorent—people want all or nothing.[3]

In the sixteenth and seventeenth centuries, these forces were augmented and intensified by vast technical and material changes. The destructiveness of warfare was increased by the invention of gunpowder; resources for paying and equipping armies were expanded through new overseas resources of gold and treasure. Because of the twin driving forces of religious fanaticism and increased material resources, the "wars of religion" in the sixteenth and seventeenth centuries came very near to wrecking Western civilization. In the late seventeenth and eighteenth centuries, religious fanaticism declined; and war in the eighteenth century became more restricted, temperate, and humane, inspiring the historian Edward Gibbon to write:

> The balance of power will continue to fluctuate, and the prosperity of our own or the neighboring kingdoms may be alternately exalted or depressed; but these events cannot essentially injure our general state of happiness, the system of arts, and laws, and manners, which so advantageously distinguish, above the rest of mankind, the Europeans and their colonies.

. . . In peace, the progress of knowledge and industry is accelerated by the emulation of so many active rivals; in war,
the European forces are exercised by temperate and undecisive contests.[4]

The nineteenth century which followed, however, was marked
not by deeper and more humane religious insights but by a negative cynicism that carried seeds of its own destruction. Fanaticism
was weakened at the cost of extinguishing religious faith. The
principle of toleration gave Western society a breathing spell, but
this period was inevitably replaced by a second epoch of fanaticism;
for it is a truism of history that man will not tolerate a spiritual
vacuum even in the form of toleration itself. The brief interlude
of more temperate international conflicts was followed by the "wars
of nationality." Logically, this was so because the spirit of man
can never be restrained from choosing faith over cynicism. Historically, it was so because any civilization including Western
civilization moves from "rout" to "rally" or from one great setback
to recovery to another more tragic relapse.

The transformation of war in the nineteenth and twentieth century thus had two aspects. In contemporary international relations,
the state assumed a new role and posture with consequences for
warfare. Princes and aristocratic governments are capable of fighting one another without excessive animosity; nations under arms
must hate each other with a consuming passion and must know
that their cause is righteous and that the threat they face is un-
paralleled aggression. The new weapons of propaganda and ideological warfare become as essential as guns and bayonets. Rivalry
and strife must be rationalized in terms of ideals and principles
rather than territorial ambitions.

The second aspect which brought about a change in warfare
was the transformation and transglorification of the state itself. For
Augustine, the state was a necessary evil. For liberalism, the state
has been the "night watchman." By the twentieth century, the
state had become the embodiment of the nation and the instrument
through which a political religion was mediated. This change in
political thought has been more far-reaching than the changes
brought about by science and technology. Modern nationalism has

an ecclesiastical tinge. In one respect, it represents a reversion to the idolatrous worship of the tribe which was the only religion known to man before the rise of the "higher religions." But the driving force of the new nationalism is a powerful religious sentiment translated into political and ideological terms. Not only is there a union between religious and ideological ideas as professed and promoted by state and nation but there is an identity. The state became religion and the religion is the state. What we have observed in Fascist Italy, Nazi Germany, and Communist Russia is merely an exaggeration of the phenomenon of political religion over large areas of the world: Iran, Pakistan, and important areas of Africa, Latin America, and the Middle East.

Alongside the intensification of strong loyalties to the nation-state and the universalizing of its mission for the world, a more recent trend has been the loss of faith in government and the state. What is true in America is being repeated throughout Europe. Indeed one possible explanation of the willingness of some European states to band together within the wider European Community is their justifiable doubt that smaller states of Europe in particular can any longer provide for the safety and well-being of their own people. Nor are the nations of Eastern Europe any longer persuaded that Soviet-style communism is the wave of the future. It is tempting but misleading to conclude that given disillusionment with government, the days of the nation-state are numbered and that transnational organizations are destined to replace nation-states. If this were so, the problems of warfare would be less acute. International organizations less affected by nationalistic fanaticism would take over conflict resolution.

Yet three decades after the ending of World War II, attitudes about government and national loyalties and political faiths appear to be following their separate and independent course. Paradoxical as it may seem, disillusionment with the state is not matched by disillusionment with nationalism. Doubts that the state can solve internal problems are voiced in the American nation where conservatives are apparently gaining increasing influence. How often do these same conservatives warn that nationalism has been (or ought to be) weakened in the struggle against communism? Instead, the selfsame spokesmen who warn of too much dependence on the state call for renewed faith in nationalism for victory in the Cold War. Their views place limits on moral disarmament in the contest with the Soviet Union. Historians of postwar American foreign policy observe that conservatives who historically have taken the lead in urging restraint in the launching of holy crusades against adversary nations have from the first days of the Cold War been in the vanguard of those who seek to mobilize the world in the struggle against international communism. And in the late 1970s once again it is conservatives who call for a resumption of ideological warfare in the East-West conflict.

Therefore, while it was argued in the 1970s that detente had replaced confrontation in Soviet-American relations and that American policy makers after John Foster Dulles had favored normalization of relations with communist and neutralist states, such pragmatic modifications in foreign policy have done little to defuse nationalistic fervor among the American people. If anyone doubts this fact, he has only to review recent American political history. Gerald Ford in campaigning for the Republican nomination for the presidency in 1976 decided to eliminate the word *detente* from his political vocabulary. When he inadvertently seemed to say in the third presidential debate with Jimmy Carter that his administration accepted the communization of Eastern Europe, he assured the election of his Democratic opponent. Similarly, the more active the principal author of detente, former secretary of state Henry Kissinger, has become politically, the less he has had to say about detente and the more he has limited the concept and hedged it about with qualifications. In 1980, the overreaction to the Soviet invasion of Afghanistan by a beleaguered President Carter desperately seeking to rebuild his political fortunes by announcing that the crisis was the most critical issue in Soviet-American relations since World War II is a third example of the continuing influence of nationalistic fervor on policy makers.

Thus nationalistic universalism—the union of nationalism with a universal political faith requiring worldwide crusades for democracy or communism—lives on into the 1980s. The more the ordinary citizen or the man in the street has come to question the viability of the state in guaranteeing social benefits and economic well-being and the more his own sense of powerlessness to achieve self-fulfillment has increased, the more he has projected his unfulfilled aspirations on the nation in international politics. His frustrations and failures individually become translated into a rather frantic and fanatical pursuit of nationalistic goals and objectives. What was true of the displaced middle class—the lumpen proletariat—in Hitler's Germany has become true of all other dissatisfied groups and ethnic minorities in their influence on present-day foreign policy. Each minority whose claims have been only partially realized within the state calls on its nation to undertake worldwide what has been denied them at home. Labor and management, blacks and Jews, Greeks and Turks, Irish and Cubans each demand and seek to implement their own militant and activist foreign policy. Each group sees itself as its own secretary of state or self-appointed presidential envoy. Far from nationalism having been transformed into internationalism, subnational groups insist that the nation's foreign policy makers do for them and their brothers abroad what they have failed to do for themselves at home. Their passion and fanaticism which had once been focused on domestic goals and objectives has been raised to the level of foreign policy, complicating the task of practical adjustments in *realpolitik* and making more difficult the pursuit of national interests than at any other time in American history.

The gravest danger, however, arises less from the clash between crusading nationalist movements than from the merging of two powerful factors, nationalism and thermonuclear weapons. At no time in the history of international relations has the need for restraint and prudence been greater. Nuclear war if it comes is more likely to result from miscalculation than calculated military actions. Yet given the worldwide struggle between the Soviet Union and the United States, the theaters for political and military interaction are more numerous than in the past. The Soviet Union and the United States, for whom the problem of Germany was once seen as the central issue in the Cold War, now confront one another in Africa, Asia, and Latin America. Each has been driven by the dynamics of the Cold War to measure world leadership not by the protection of vital national interest but by success or failure in peripheral international conflicts around the globe. Internationalism which was once conceived as the palliative of local conflicts has instead become the battleground for victory or defeat everywhere around the world. The inevitable rivalry between the two great powers has been magnified by the revolutions in transportation and communications into a universal struggle. When tensions erupt or warfare threatens anywhere in the world, local and national leaders call on the United States and the Soviet Union to come to their aid. The miracle of instantaneous communications has decreed that day or night the president or the Soviet premier are summoned to affirm American or Soviet policy for each impending crisis. World leadership is equated for the two superpowers with initiatives and actions everywhere in the world. Everyone's business has become Soviet and American business, in part because of the requirements of power and in part because of the transformation of foreign-policy objectives into moral crusades conducted around the world electronically.

Internationalism and nationalism interact as well in the changing character of the international economy. The economic power of the largest corporations exceeds the gross national products of most of the 150 sovereign nation states. The multinational corporations conduct more or less independent foreign policies on all major continents and in numerous independent states. Each has in effect its own state department, its own political and economic advisors who help it chart its course. The large corporations have economic objectives that are convergent in some respects with the foreign-policy objectives of their parent states. In other respects, their objectives diverge from the foreign policies of their states of incorporation. For example, the economic objectives of most giant corporations include the avoidance of nationalization of their branches in other countries. Their parent states may seek to protect them and may establish codes of investment practice that guard against the arbitrary seizure of their assets in foreign countries. At the same time, a nation's need for allies may lead to its adopting more conciliatory attitudes toward national controls in foreign countries and even partial nationalization of assets. What the corporation considers fair business practices when it calls for opposition to what is described as unethical nationalization by foreign governments gives corporations motivations which may conflict with national motivations to have friendly relations with the host country in which its corporations invest. It is illusory, in other words, to believe that corporate objectives are always identical with foreign-policy objectives.

The unique role of transnational corporations in international relations is a product of two other factors. The one is their scale and magnitude, their sheer size and the extent of their influence. The other is their worldwide mission. Whatever their national homes, their functions cross national boundaries.

Given the economic power of multinational corporations, the political power they can exercise at important centers of decision making in foreign policy would be difficult to exaggerate. The assumption that all important decisions are made by the leaders of sovereign nation-states as stated in the traditional literature of international politics must be qualified. Economic data demonstrates that the productive activities of certain of the world's largest firms is substantially greater than the equivalent GNP-measure for many small and relatively less developed smaller countries. A giant utility such as American Telephone and Telegraph produces more than do the entire economies of countries such as Greece, Israel, Norway, and Venezuela—countries which are generally considered to have significant influence in the United Nations and international politics in general. Manufacturing firms specializing in vehicles and consumer durables (General Motors) and oil (Exxon) produce more than do the total national economies of Ireland, New Zealand, or Pakistan.[5]

The size of the international work force of a number of multinational corporations and the proportion of their foreign to total earnings clearly indicates the extent of their international as distinct from national interests. One index reports: "As long ago as 1970, one-third of the work force of several hundred multinationals surveyed by the Department of Commerce were employed abroad. In a survey of manufacturing firms, the ratio was 29.8 percent of the work force at the end of 1969 and 34 percent at the end of

1973."[6] By 1979, the figure had increased proportionately. In 1974, the foreign earnings of American multinationals accounted for 26.9 percent of their total earnings, up from 8.6 percent in 1957.

Some observers pointing to these or similar factors have argued that the expanding power of the multinationals in relation to that of important nation-states has altered the map of international politics. Concepts like transnational relations and an interdependent world have crept into discussions of international order and the structure of international relations. Without detracting from the importance of the new transnational actors including but not limited to multinational corporations, this trend of thought requires qualification. In international politics, economic power is not always translated into political power. The multinationals, because of their rather precarious position in highly nationalistic states, must proceed with restraint and caution. The engines of political power still remain national governments which continue to control decision making on issues of vital interests. It should not be forgotten that the far-reaching decisions on energy and pricing policy made in 1973 at the time of the oil boycott were not those of multinational corporations but of important Middle Eastern states. The governments of Iran, Saudi Arabia, Kuwait, and Libya, not OPEC as a transnational energy body, decreed that prices and allocations should be made in the interests of the oil-producing states. The unified policies of OPEC gave such decisions a weight that a single nation's policies might not have achieved. Yet the source of the decisions was national policy making, which OPEC coordinated and unified into a common strategic course of action.

Therefore, the most accurate description of the international environment is one that calls attention to both its national and international dimensions. In the same way that state actions and free enterprise exist side by side in most of the developed economies, nationalism and internationalism are the two elements that constitute the international system. To stress one and ignore the other is to distort the true picture of contemporary international relations. Only the naïve and the half-informed observer would claim that nationalism was dead. At the same time, it is misleading to believe that the actions of large transnational bodies have no influence on international politics. The unique characteristic of the international system which sets it apart from earlier systems is its essential dualism. Every chief executive, including the president of the United States, must come to terms with the two dimensions of the present international order. In an attempt to be progressively international, he cannot gloss over the residual importance of national concerns and constraints. He has no choice between pursuing the national interest and some other form of foreign policy. His responsibilities are determined by his oath of office and his mandate to safeguard his country's vital interests. Having accepted this responsibility and being guided by it, he simultaneously needs to recognize the new dimensions of international relations. What political scientists define as "the influentials" in politics and international politics include for him powerful new transnational actors who may forge networks of relations that shape the changing international order. It would be as fallacious to reject constraints of nationalism as it would to pass over the growing authority of transnational activities and relationships. A perspective of "both-and" provides a sounder basis for international thought and action than one of "either-or."

We are told that the president must exercise world leadership because the United States is the world's most powerful nation. If one can learn from the experience of the three decades following World War II, however, one lesson from this era is surely the limits of American power. The illusion we carried into the postwar era was that America was omnipotent. From having been a power which threw its weight onto the balance at the eleventh hour, we became the determining factor in (almost) every nation's calculation of the world's distribution of power. If some liberals and a few conservatives found Henry Luce's coinage of the phrase "the American Century" too vainglorious, the nation's consensus on foreign-policy objectives was not far removed. Implementing the Truman Doctrine and defending freedom around the world were only a little less universalistic than Mr. Luce's grand design.

The years of the Cold War and its most serious crises threw a shadow over the towering vision of those who equated world leadership with the country's omnipotence. Americans found that, however powerful, the nation could not work its will on smaller states to achieve all its ends either through political coercion or military action. The limits of America's authority can be traced on a line running from Berlin to Korea to Cuba and to Vietnam. If it is true American power must be accounted for in every major struggle anywhere in the world, it is also true that such power however great hardly assures that America can always have its way. American hegemony has been thrown into question not by the fainthearted within but by events in the world outside the United States.

Why then the continuing assumption of America's omniscience and absolute power? What are the roots of the belief that we are and can be everywhere supreme? In part this illusion is a consequence of a confusion of technology and policy. The common assumption in both the United States and the Soviet Union has been that the revolutions in communications and transportation have transformed the character of international relations. Satellites hovering over the earth enable the great powers to transmit instantaneously their messages around the world. The conversion of mankind to democracy or communism, which had been impossible at the time of Wilson and Lenin, is now quite conceivable through modern science. The means being available, the public assumes that the possibility of sustaining or reshaping other political systems is readily at hand. Soviet leaders speak of helping national liberation movements to gain their legitimate ends; the United States views itself as the champion of human rights throughout the world. These objectives are differently defined than those of Wilson and Lenin but fundamentally they involve the same ultimate ends: the extension of democracy and communism wherever possible to every corner of the globe. True believers on both sides look forward to the day when the world will have peace, freedom, and justice through the spreading of cherished ideals and structures. If one side is more fanatical and less open to diversity, both hold to their beliefs out of conviction and self-assurance that their goals are best for the world.

The other way a president or a Soviet premier can approach the question of world leadership is through pursuing the concept

of the national interest. Nations, however powerful, remain limited
in what they can do in the world. As individuals, nations must
decide what is more and less vital to their cause. As Walter Lippmann put it, they must bring their commitments and their power
into balance. No nation can do everything its leaders dream of
doing in and for the world. They must relate what is desirable to
what is necessary and possible. Technology and science are boundless in their outreach and potential; politics is the art of the possible taking place within determinate if changeable boundaries.
American political and intellectual leaders have opened the door
to disillusionment and despair by imagining that the potentialities
of science were equatable with the possibilities of politics.

Therefore success for any chief executive responsible for conducting his nation's relations with other peoples, and especially for
the president of the mightiest world power, is to recover a sense of
the connection between world leadership and the national interest.
He must seek that connection through a better understanding of
internationalism and nationalism as they constitute the structure
of the contemporary world order. In his search, those who serve
him best will be advisors and thinkers who point to the duality of
the international system. In his policies, he must find practical
and realistic approaches to problems that fall more clearly into one
or the other sector. His choices will not only be open to analysis
and decision by men of thought and ideas; his actions will also
be judged by historians for their consequences for man's survival.
This setting for world leadership is one that great leaders not only
understand intellectually but feel in the marrow of their bones.
Those who guide the nation through its most fateful days will be
those who take hold of great issues within a well understood
framework; those who fail will be those who remain amateurs and
innocents about the baffling and oftentimes contradictory trends of
internationalism and nationalism.

Two quotations summarize and pull together all that we have
said. The first is a statement by the former Indonesian ambassador
to the United States, Soedjatmoko:

It is very important to study the United States Presidency
not only in its relationship to the bureaucracy in the United

States, to the party system, or to Congress, or in the way it is itself organized, but it should also be studied in its transnational aspect. There is almost no decision which the U.S. President takes that has no transnational impact. This may be in terms of the general perception of the public abroad regarding U.S. leadership capacity or its absence, but also on the money market and on the calculations of anyone involved in the global and local power game. The foreign perspectives which shape the perceptions of the American Presidency are often determined by historical and cultural factors. These have to be studied as well, if we want to have a better understanding of the impact of the U.S. Presidency in the world.[7]

The other comes from Hans J. Morgenthau, America's leading theorist of international politics:

Good motives give assurance against deliberately bad policies; they do not guarantee the moral goodness and political success of the policies they inspire. What is important to know, if one wants to understand foreign policy, is not primarily the motives of a statesman, but his intellectual ability to comprehend the essentials of foreign policy, as well as his political ability to translate what he has comprehended into successful political action.[8]

For contemporary statesmen, Morgenthau urged as a guidepost the following principle:

Statesmen, especially under contemporary conditions, may well make a habit of presenting their foreign policies in terms of their philosophic and political sympathies in order to gain popular support for them. Yet they will distinguish with Lincoln between their *"official* duty," which is to think and act in terms of the national interest, and their *"personal* wish," which is to see their own moral values and political principles realized throughout the world.[9]

It is the essence of the difference between moralistic universalism and a foreign policy, that the statesman concentrate on the distinction between what is required for the state, what is desirable and what is possible, what is necessary and what may be ideally good. Interests, not ideals, tend to dominate the actions of men and even for a transnational world such interests must be reckoned with in reconciling internationalism and nationalism.

Writing of the new international economic order, Leopold S. Amery observed: "The basis and starting point of such a system must be the nation, namely the unit of political and legislative action, of taxation, of social and defensive policy—above all the unit of sentiment."[10] If the nation remains the channel through which international commitments are implemented, it remains vital for policy makers and scholars to give attention to the imperatives of national interest even in an era of transnationalism. Groups with transnational relations turn in the end to national governments for achievement of their ends. American agriculture urges its government to favor an international regime of free trade so it can export its products while European farmers call on their governments to protect them from lower priced agricultural imports. The food problem has become worldwide but its resolution involves national policies, at least in the first instance. It is often the case that some nations are able to cloak their uniquely national interests in the language of wider transnational interests, leading Charles Kindleberger to write: "One can envy the special interest which is able to clothe its arguments in general terms while other special groups whose interests cannot be identified with the Commonwealth, are obliged to either cling to patently thin general arguments or reveal themselves as selfish."[11]

Therefore, the focus must be on action ,more than ideology in relating nationalism and internationalism. Where are the decisions made, especially the controlling ones? Nations like individuals may claim to follow a transcendent cause. The task is to look for operative ideas and principles which govern their relationship with one another.

II Public Philosophy Renewed: Ideas, Institutions, and Ideologies

4

The Quest for a
Public Philosophy

In continuing this analysis of the presidency and the public philosophy I would like to focus on three provocative texts. Walter Lippmann wrote in one of his earliest essays:

> We expect of one man that he shall speak for the nation, formulate its needs, translate them into a program. We expect that man to instill these purposes and this program into a parasitic party system, drive his own party to enact them, and create an untainted administrative hierarchy through which to realize his plans. We expect him to oversee the routine, dominate group interests, prepare for the future, and take stock of possible emergencies. No man can do it.[1]

The second text is revisionist. A colleague is reported to have reworded the famed "salvation by staff" injunction of the President's Committee on Administrative Management of 1937: "The President needs help" to read: "The President doesn't need help" or more specifically doesn't need "too much help of the wrong kind."

A third text is more current. It is contained in a two-part *Atlantic Monthly* article by a former Carter speech writer, James Fallows, still loyal but seeking to explain why a president "who would surely outshine most other leaders in the judgment of the Lord," had failed to win support for his programs: "I came to think," Fallows writes, "that Carter believes fifty things, but no one thing. He holds . . . positions on every issue under the sun, but he has no large view of the relations between them, no line

indicating which goals . . . will take predecence over which . . .
when the goals conflict. Spelling out these choices makes the difference between a position and a philosophy, but it is an act
foreign to Carter's mind. . . . Values that others would find contradictory complement one another in his mind. During the campaign he used to say that our nation was the first to provide 'complete compatibility' between liberty and equality. This pained me
. . . I told him . . . the tensions between them shape most of American society. . . . Carter thinks in lists, not arguments; as long as
the items are there, their order does not matter, nor does the
hierarchy among them."[2] Nonetheless, Fallows, who is surely a
friendly critic, concludes he would vote for Carter for reelection
as the best available candidate.

The three quotations suggest three broad themes that interrelate and affect one another in this transitional era in the history
of the American presidency. They are: the concept of the presidency; the organization of the presidency; the public philosophy
and the presidency.

THE CONCEPT OF THE PRESIDENCY

Debates over ruling concepts of the presidency have divided thinkers since the founding of the Republic. Among the fathers, some
preferred a king but others feared monarchy. Some warned of a
powerless executive, others of usurpation of Congress' powers.
Alexander Hamilton called for an energetic executive, if not a
constitutional monarch. Thomas Jefferson feared that hereditary
power might result if presidents could be reelected. John Adams
wrote Jefferson: "You are apprehensive of monarchy; I of aristocracy. I would therefore have given more power to the President
and less to the Senate." But Abraham Lincoln declared: "I have
been selected to fill an important office for a brief period. . . .
Should my administration prove to be a very wicked one, or what
is more probable a very foolish one, if you, the people are true
to yourselves and the Constitution, there is but little harm I can
do, thank God."

The gulf between theory and practice, words and deeds of the presidency illuminates differences in concepts. Jefferson's apprehension of monarchical power did not stand in the way of his initiating the Louisiana Purchase, an act of unrivaled executive energy ratified because of Jefferson's consummate political skills with the Congress. Lincoln raised an army before the Congress had declared war. Woodrow Wilson carried the fight for the League of Nations to the people, bypassing the Senate. Theodore Roosevelt saw in the presidency "a bully pulpit." For him, as for Wilson and FDR, the concept of the presidency included a vision of the president as popular leader, educator, and teacher.

The vision of the president as teacher always has appealed to some Americans while being offensive to others. There are those who believe that if the people are not virtuous, presidential preachments will make them so. The leader single-handedly will purge the public of its sins and move society from selfishness to virtue, from apathy to action, from debauchery to righteousness. We especially revere those presidents who taught by both precept and example: Washington, national independence; Jefferson, benevolence and happiness; and Lincoln, preservation of the union and binding up the wounds.

This activist vision of leadership competes with Edmund Burke's classic view that the leader's task is "to follow, not force the public inclination, to give a direction, a form, a technical dress, and a specific sanction, to the general sense of community. The general sense of the community may wait to be aroused, and the statesman may arouse it; it may be inchoate and vague, and the statesman must formulate it and make it explicit."[3] The younger Woodrow Wilson as political theorist understood this and wrote: "Society is not a crowd, but an organism, and like every organism, it must grow as a whole. . . . This organic whole, Society . . . must grow by the development of its aptitudes and desires." The leader must guide the slow-paced daily needs of the people, and the young Wilson warned: "In no case may we safely hurry the organism away from its habit: for it is held together by that habit. Society must walk, dependent upon practicable paths, incapable of scaling sudden precipitous heights, a roadbreaker not a fowl of the air."

The president who would teach must be a roadbreaker, must understand society and its habits, and must demonstrate his understanding to the people. If he is seen to be unschooled, naïve, or innocent of society and the realities of governance, he will fail as a teacher, however noble his ideals.

Furthermore, a contemporary president who would educate the people does so against mounting odds. As problems and politics have grown more complex, recent presidents have faced greater political and practical difficulties in mobilizing the nation, leading some to quote Jefferson's dictum: "Great innovations should not be forced on slender majorities." Changes in the political process with political parties having less to say about presidential selection have weakened the capacity of any president to teach and lead, and have weakened his call on party loyalties in implementing his policies. Dr. James Ceaser has argued in an authoritative study of presidential selection that the brokerage function of the parties and of party leadership in choosing a candidate capable of holding together diverse party elements has been superseded by the instant judgment of the media, by unending popular plebiscites in presidential primaries and by a proliferation of fractional group and minority representation ethically defensible but politically damaging, especially in the Democratic party nominating conventions. In 1976, a television professional, Sander Vanocur, wrote:

> In an age where the medium has become the political process, it sets the stage, assigns all the roles and tells us when we should laugh and . . . cry. It has become our Greek chorus, mocking any attempts at reasoned political discourse. . . . What used to count in presidential campaigns was political muscle—organization, canvassing phone banks. . . . The political process is too complicated, at times even too mystical an experience for a medium that is designed . . . to make brief claims on our attention spans. We have heard . . . that it has been a lackluster campaign devoid of any issues. But who is responsible? It is not the candidates. They would be fools if they tried to explore issues in a medium that measures out the world in 30-second takes.[4]

Add one further difficulty or constraint, the tenfold expansion of new centers of power in Congress with some 150 aspiring subcommittee chairmen each seeking a place in the sun and replacing 12 to 15 all-powerful senior committee chairmen, and the review is complete.

Yet the root causes of the present political crisis are deeper and more fundamental than the effects of the media, and of popularity contests in the primaries, of minority representation in nominating conventions, and of scores of aspiring new congressional leaders vying for recognition and power. What Lippman's warning foreshadowed and what Wilson's image of society as an organic whole never anticipated are a clustering of social developments that have thrown up roadblocks for any president and impediments to every historic concept of the office. The shining example America offered the world of unity in diversity—*e pluribus unum*—has been fractured in our times. Diversity has outrun unity with the rise of countless little special-interest or single-interest groups, politically influential and controlling the balance of power. In the 1960s, the nation was concerned that society was running roughshod over marginal men and women, the forgotten people in democracy. Today serious commentators are sounding an alarm that new marginal groups or groups who try to prove they are marginal have come to dominate the nation's political process. For every truth, wrote Lord Acton, there is a balancing truth, and today's truth is the need for balancing individual's special interests and ethnic rights with a revitalized concept of the public interest with new content for the times, continually reordered, broadened, and redefined to include minority rights. This theme links any discussion of the concept of the presidency with the idea of a public philosophy.

THE ORGANIZATION OF THE PRESIDENCY

Each president imposes his own organizational system onto the office, but there are also trends and historical tendencies. Paul H. Nitze writes on this theme in a recently published Miller Center Forum devoted to policy making by the eight presidents whom he served during four decades. Nitze favors transferring back some or all of the staff functions that have been going to the White House to the operating departments saying, "Frankly, I think

the White House staff is too big, deals with too many diverse
questions and isn't focused on central issues." He concludes: "The
main problem with the presidency is the economy of time. What
we have is one man with a twelve hour day. . . . How do you prevent everything going to the President? I think you prevent it
mainly through decentralization of authority. In the Truman
years . . . the great factor was Mr. Truman's confidence in General
Marshall, Dean Acheson, Robert Lovett and a few others"—confidence which gave them credibility in speaking and acting for
him.[5]

In 1937, the President's Committee on Administrative Management declared in its report, "The President needs help." The
growth of presidential responsibilities led to the formation in
1939 of the Executive Office. For several generations of scholars
and a series of government reorganization plans, the words of the
committee became sacred doctrine. By the 1970s, the presidency
had become a command post for policy initiatives, an overseer of
all government operations, and a managerial and operational
agency. Franklin Roosevelt's White House staff consisted of 45
employees in 1938; by 1960 there were nearly 300 staff positions
in the Executive Office of the president, and Jimmy Carter employs nearly 600 White House advisors. According to Thomas E.
Cronin, the president now needs help to manage his helpers.[6] The
Executive Office alone exceeds in size and function the entire civil
government during Jefferson's presidency. It has doubled since
World War II. Cabinet members complain of being pushed around
by White House staff. Lost somehow along the way were reasonable efforts to distinguish tasks that only the president can perform
from efforts more appropriately undertaken by others. The great
debate which is forming among presidential scholars focuses on the
role of the president's aides as the chief managers of the federal
government, a role few would claim can be traced to the Constitution. A forty-year trend with its beginnings in the Roosevelt presidency has come under fire. The centralization of power in the White
House once viewed as a solution to all problems has come to be seen
as a source of many of our difficulties in society. Executive-legislative
councils and more effective use of a strong cabinet are being pro-

posed as alternatives to the governing of the country by young and inexperienced presidential advisors.

Presidential scholars who sound the alarm and find illness in the body politic have a responsibility to prescribe as well as to diagnose. In this regard, any administration seeking a valid framework for organizing the presidency might be wise to consider what my colleague James S. Young has called constitutionalism and presidentialism, two classic terms that he defines as follows:

> Constitutionalism means a slow-moving system that invites contention in public decision making and generously distributes the power of veto among the participants. It means a system that depends on consensus, prefers the risk of deadlock to the risks of reliance on a powerful leader, and pays the price of many little governments to avoid the costs of tyranny. Presidentialism means a White House empowered to cut through that system or break out of it. It means a Presidency equipped to monitor those forces, here and broad, that critically affect the conditions of American life, and to step in and change them when discontent or danger threatens to rend the Republic or end it.[7]

Until recently, America was successful in maintaining these two patterns of governance avoiding the risks of arbitrary rule and tyranny through constitutionalism and of deadlock in crises through presidentialism. Presidentialism provided a contingency system to remedy delays in constitutionalism; it was addressed to meeting extraordinary needs.

To restore a tenuous harmony between constitutionalism and presidentialism, leading American scholars have called for retrenching presidential power in order to preserve it, winding down presidential government to save it for what only it can do. They have urged presidential self-restraint distinguishing between what are true and pseudo-crises or threats to the Republic and mere problems for a particular administration. Professor Young has prescribed "getting the Presidency substantially out of the business of managing the executive branch: ceding large parts of that domain to Congress, courts and cabinet, but not ceding the President's power to preempt or intervene when reasons of state require it."[8]

These proposals constitute a worthwhile agenda for national

discussion and for the ongoing study of the presidency. Proponents acknowledge they have not provided a magical blueprint that gives automatic answers to stubborn and intractable problems of choice. The imperatives of wise statecraft and of knowing instinctively "when to step in and when to stay out" have increased, not diminished. But leaders pondering the requirements of organization had better reflect on the need for new frameworks when old frameworks are a part of the crisis of the presidency.

THE PUBLIC PHILOSOPHY AND THE PRESIDENCY

Having reflected on the concept of the presidency and the organization of the presidency, we come inevitably to the necessity for a working philosophy to form and guide the complex and versatile role that is the president's. Lacking such a philosophy, any president responds to separate problems within water-tight compartments and the citizen is bereft of anchors for thought and action. As in Lincoln's time, the public is "bereft of faith but terrified by doubt." Paradoxically, a public philosophy was more nearly within reach in the founding days of the Republic when concern for political ideas of lasting value enjoyed an early flowering by men whom Charles Beard described as "richer in political experience and in practical knowledge . . . endowed with a profounder insight into the springs of human action and the . . . essence of government" than at any time in history. Walter Lippmann toward the end of his life confessed to a British audience that America lacked a common philosophy and undertook in his last major work, *The Public Philosophy*, to provide one. It is easier to describe the elements essential to a public philosophy than to achieve consensus on them. For the scaffolding what is needed are, first, certain bedrock principles on the nature of man, of politics, of society, and of the nation-state including its relations with other states; and, second, concepts of governance, of the public interest, and the common good which transcends private interests.

If it is accepted that the perennial problem of democratic leaders is to establish a viable and lasting framework of values and that failure to do so leads to loss of public support, the question is where are leaders to discover such a framework. A debate among theorists and practitioners, pundits, and policy makers on this question has continued down to the present. It is argued that Theodore Roosevelt's working framework was too jingoistic and nationalistic although, as his relations with Andrew Carnegie suggest, he entertained ideas about universal disarmament which he subordinated in the concrete policies he pursued. Woodrow Wilson saw the United States in the vanguard of a movement for a new world in which national purposes would fall more and more into the background. His framework was in part responsible for turning him away from necessary concern for territorial and political questions on which the security of Europe continued to be based. Franklin D. Roosevelt, the consummate national politician, may have been misled by his domestic political successes into believing that international diplomacy across ideological lines was less intractable than it proved to be. In seeking to internationalize certain national values in a partly anarchic world society, he may have been only the first of a succession of presidents who sought to transfer a moral framework appropriate to America but not to the rest of the world.

In the search for a moral framework that would guide our leaders and lend continuity to the policy making of the nation, two contending schools of thought about national and international values have advanced opposing viewpoints: a natural-law viewpoint, or something close to it, and a viewpoint which looks to earlier American traditions of political thought as correctives to popular, contemporary views. Both viewpoints appear far removed from political necessities in an era of electronic politics. Neither is easily translated from theory into practice. Yet, if discussions of presidential leadership are to be more than occasions for praise and blame, attention must be given to political theory no less than to political tactics.

Natural-law teachings look for fixed points in the moral and political universe. While understanding of such political truths is reserved to the political philosopher, these principles are approximated in different degrees within separate political systems and are to be appropriated through reason. For our purposes, natural-law systems of thought appear less relevant than modified natural-law teachings. Thus Walter Lippmann wrote in *The Public Philosophy*:

> I have been arguing, hopefully and wishfully, that it may be
> possible to alter the terms of discourse if a convincing demon-
> stration can be made that the principles of the good society
> are not in Sartre's phrase, invented and chosen—that the con-
> ditions which must be met if there is to be a good society are
> there, outside our wishes, where they can be discovered by ra-
> tional inquiry, and adapted and refined by rational discus-
> sion.[9]

The criticism of natural-law thinking has focused on its over-
dependence on reason. There is an essential irrationality to politics
which Paul Valery defined when he asserted that politicians "deny,
in order to survive, what they promised in order to get a start."
Political necessities, we are told, "oblige us to say emphatically
what we could not possibly think, to promise the impossible, to
speculate on credulity . . . to reckon with fools, to flatter people
who repel us, to deprecate the man we esteem—all this for the
sake of winning or keeping power, whose possession in every
imaginable case will be an experience of helplessness." Natural-
law theorists have faced difficulties in coming to terms with the
ambiguities and contradictions of politics. If virtue is the highest
end of man, his virtue hardly remains untarnished in his pursuit
of power. A further problem is the persistent need for the followers
of natural law to adapt fixed norms to the complex realities of
daily life as in a recent report that the Archdiocese of New York
had joined in a trend begun in many other American dioceses.
In ministering to divorced Roman Catholics, the archdiocese is
sponsoring seminars on how Catholics can cope with divorce, receive the sacraments, and remarry with the Church's blessing. What
is true in the community of the family is true to a still greater
extent in the international community where in Reinhold Niebuhr's words there is no single norm, whether peace or justice or
freedom, by which other norms can be ordered.

Another viewpoint stems from earlier American political
thought. The nation's political theory enjoyed an early flowering
particularly in its insights regarding the nature of man, the char-

acter of representative government, the importance of national unity, the place of the higher law, and the value of a wise dispersion and balancing of power. The founders, it is true, did not have a simple view of human nature. They are sometimes depicted as enlightment enthusiasts who saw the universe and the process of government in mechanical terms, or as disillusioned Puritans who preached self-restraint but no longer believed in it, or as Whig politicians suspicious of all power, or as elite cynics who feared the ignorance and dissatisfaction of the masses. They were all of these things and more. They saw human nature as complex and varied, affected by habit, reason, economics, and faith, in need of guidance and deserving freedom. They offered no final answers. Adams and Jefferson spent their last years in serious reflection and debate about the same issues which preoccupied their public careers. They engaged early and late in moral and political reasoning and thus provide, even for our day, maxims of political wisdom.

The value of their political thought is disputed by some present-day political theorists. John Roche describes the federal convention as a "reform caucus in action," lacking any special theoretical or moral significance. He speaks of the Constitution as "a patch work sewn together under the pressure of both time and events by a group of extremely talented democratic politicians. . . . For over three months, in what must have seemed to the faithful participants an endless process of give and take, they reasoned, cajoled, threatened and bargained amongst themselves. . . . The Constitution was neither a victory for abstract theory nor a great practical success."[10] The late Columbia University historian Richard Hofstadter sees the origin of many American political problems in the limitations of the founders' understanding of human nature. He wrote:

> To them a human being was an atom of self-interest. They did not believe in man, but they did believe in the power of a good political constitution to control him. . . . From a humanistic standpoint there is a serious dilemma in the philosophy of the Fathers, which derives from their conception of man. They thought man was a creature of rapacious self-interest, yet they wanted him to be free—free, in essence, to contend, to engage in an umpired strife, to use property to get

property. . . . They had no hope and they offered none for any ultimate organic change in the way men conduct themselves. The result was that while they thought self-interest the most dangerous and unbrookable quality of man, they necessarily underwrote it in trying to control it.[11]

According to this view, the problems that confound present-day American politics of special-interest groups and materialism are not problems the founding fathers can answer; they expected such groups to exist and saw politics merely as a balancing of and bargaining among private interests; what's more, the founders have a view of human nature that is of little relevance because of its pessimism and the fact it was designed to legitimate capitalism.

One defense of the founders is that of the late Martin Diamond, who argued, in support of the commercial virtues, that acquisitiveness is a higher virtue than avarice; it involves a discipline, a willingness to work, and a concern for the future of society. It involves, in other words, something more than gouging your neighbor. In Alexander Hamilton's words, America would nurture "the assiduous merchant the laborious husbandman, the active mechanic, and the industrious manufacturer." In Hannah Arendt's words, there is a distinction between the drudgery of labor and the vocation of work. For Alex de Tocqueville, "self-interest properly understood" was the motivating force for a wide range of social and political cooperation in the United States. He hoped that the United States would be an example through which "a kind of virtuous materialism may ultimately be established in the world, which would not corrupt, but enervate the soul, and noiselessly unbend its springs of action."[12]

However, there is another defense of the founders that can be made without simply praising or justifying commerce and materialism. Though they formed their government with the realistic expectation that "enlightened statesmen will not always be at the helm" (*Federalist* No. 10) and the conviction that it is more secure to use "opposite and rival interests" to prevent tyranny than to depend on the presence of "better motives" (*Federalist* No. 51), the founders also understood the connection between private virtue and the public good. According to Thomas Jefferson: "It is the manners and spirit of a people which preserve a republic in vigor. A degeneracy in these is a canker which soon eats into the heart of its laws and constitution." Washington's Farewell Address affirmed that "virtue or morality is a necessary spring of popular government."[13] Virtue was a precondition of liberty; and in Jefferson's highest hopes, if not his realistic expectations, republican government based on virtue would promote the development of a natural aristocracy and the rise of that aristocracy to political power. What the citizens do at home was important to the nation's influence abroad; for in John C. Calhoun's words, we "do more to extend liberty by our example over this continent and this world generally than would be done by a thousand victories."[14]

The founders, in summary, thought that the subject of morality was of immense importance. Sometimes their ideas were linked with commerce and industriousness; as in Franklin's words: "The almost general Mediocrity of Fortune that prevails in America obliging its People to follow some Business for subsistence, those Vices, that arise from Idleness, are in great measure prevented."[15] Yet John Adams wrote of the ambiguous effects of work—favorable in emulation, unfavorable in envy and jealousy. Comparing the good and the bad in industriousness, he declared: "This propensity [for comparison] . . . is a principal source of the virtues and vices, the happiness and misery of human life; and the history of mankind is little more than a simple narration of its operation and effects."[16] Or while recognizing the place of national self-respect and pride in politics, Adams explained: "Power always thinks it has a great soul and vast views beyond the comprehension of the weak and that it is doing God's service when it is violating all His laws. Our passions, ambitions, avarice, love, and resentment, etc. possess so much metaphysical subtlety and so much overpowering eloquence that they insinuate themselves into the understanding and the conscience and convert both to their party."

Whatever the deficiencies of the founders, they offer political insights on power and work, virtue and justice, ambiguity and proportion that is often missing from contemporary discourse. Our present problems are rooted less in the structure of democratic government, though democracy has its limitations, and more in the pervasive shallowness of the culture fostered by our growing dependence on the media, by our methods of presidential selection, by the consequences of recent events to which we not only react but may overreact, by the complexities of public issues like inflation, energy, and women's rights, and by the inordinate power of special-interest groups. The response to this shallowness is to elevate somehow the level of public debate and to revive the habit of moral reasoning by, in part at least, reminding ourselves of the political thought of the founding fathers—their view of human nature, their discourse on morality in politics, and their political practice which was in some respects superior to our own.

In the current era, the main road for attaining rising economic and social expectations leads to Washington and especially to the president, the only man elected by all the people. Every group or interest turns to the president not for help with the general welfare but for help to the poor, the sick, the aged, big business, small business, organized labor, the cities, the farmers, education, and countless other groups. No president can give any group all it wants and therefore no president can retain everyone's favor. Aspirations and appetites have grown contradictory and insatiable: citizens want tax relief or a guaranteed annual income; big business, big railroads, and big cities all oppose intervention but want a bailout. The president becomes the focal point of every hope and expectation of every group in the Republic.

One way to protect the president is to scale down the organization of the White House or unrealistic concepts of what any president can do. The other way is to raise up and rediscover certain truths that were once part of the fabric of American society, were in fact the public philosophy. Confronting the present malaise in higher political and constitutional values a former secretary of state asks: "Where have all the citizens gone? Where are those who think of themselves first as members of this great Republic, whose own particular interests cannot thrive unless this Nation survives and flourishes?"[17]

A contemporary public philosophy, if it were possible, would have to do more, however, than applaud the common good. It would have to set forth those rock-bottom beliefs which in their interrelationships help men understand themselves, the political process, and America's place in the world. Its starting point, as with all philosophy, would have to be man's most vexing problem: himself, a being neither wholly good nor evil but one in whom curiously intermingled are elements of the divine and the demonic. Man who is capable of doing so much good is also capable of self-deception about his own interests and power. To repeat John Adams' words: "Power always thinks it has a great soul and vast views . . . [and] is doing God's service when it is violating all his laws." In another context, Adams prophesied: "The language of nature to man in his constitution is this—'I have given you reason, conscience, and benevolence; and thereby made you accountable for your actions, and capable of virtue, in which you will fill your highest felicity. But I have not confided wholly in your laudable improvement of these divine gifts. To them I have superadded in your bosoms a passion for the notice and regard of your fellow mortals, which, if you perversely violate your duty, and wholly neglect the part assigned you in the system of the world and the society of mankind, shall torture you from the cradle to the grave." The founders understood this strange intermingling of responsibility and selfish passions and created a government of checks and balances to safeguard against the pretentions of power. They went back to Montesquieu, who argued that there can be no liberty when executive and legislative power are united in one person. In *Federalist* No. 51, James Madison wrote: "It may be a reflection on human nature that such devices (checks and balances) should be necessary to control the abuses of government. But what is government . . . but the greatest of all reflections on human nature. If men were angels, no government would be necessary. If angels were to govern men, neither external nor internal controls on government would be necessary."

Yet overarching the checks and balances among the branches of government and the divisions of federalism, was a pantheon of higher values embodied in the Bill of Rights and reflecting common interests. The founders, whatever their social origins, be-

lieved that government and law were intended to serve the whole
society. Loyalties to separate interests and communities were morally tolerable only when they included values wider than those communities, whether the village, the state, or the nation. Individuals
and nations alike, to bring legitimacy to their interests, were to
use power as an instrument of justice and a servant of interests
broader than their own. The process of moral reasoning, not the
listing of good causes, was the method by which higher and lower
values and priorities of interest could be established. Moral and
political choices would always be difficult and frequently painful:
freedom of speech and assembly versus denying men the right to
cry fire in a crowded theater, a fair trial versus the rights of the
public, freedom versus order, liberty versus equality, security versus
individual rights, economic growth versus environmentalism, peace
versus justice, stability versus progress, the rights of landlords
versus tenants, or of majorities versus minorities. Every individual
who has agonized over harsh choices involving devotion to wife and
family versus responsibility to aging parents, or professional commitments versus parental responsibilities has known something of
the anguish and sacrifices of moral choice. Yet how many of our
leaders help us to see that the demands of political choice are not
easy but heroic, and have a tragic dimension with which we must
learn to live?

Finally, a public philosophy would leave room for a contemporary statement of the principles of republican and representative
government, which from the founding have provided the setting
for American democracy. Representative government has assumed
that trust will be reposed in chosen leaders of whom at their best
it could be said, as Thucydides said of Pericles: "He enjoyed so
high a reputation that he could afford to anger them by contradiction. . . . With his successors it was different. More on a level with
one another, and each grasping at supremacy, they ended by com-
mitting . . . state affairs to the whims of the multitudes." Or stating
the decline in another way: "Being a man of great power both for
his dignity and wisdom, and for bribes manifestly the most incor-
rupt, he freely controlled the multitude and was not so much led
by them as he led them. . . . But they that came after, being more

equal amongst themselves and affecting everyone to be the chief, applied themselves to the people and let go the care of the commonwealth."[18]

Edmund Burke in his address of November 3, 1774, to the Electors of Bristol declared that he would betray his public trust if he subordinated his judgment to their opinions on issues for which his position and responsibility afforded him greater knowledge and understanding. James Madison in *Federalist* No. 10 held out the hope that "the public voice, pronounced by the representatives of the people, will be more consonant to the public good than if pronounced by the people themselves." Thus a modern public philosophy must make room for a restatement of public trust in our leaders. Especially with questions requiring years of study or extraordinary intellectual and professional competence or decisions that cannot be delayed, it is asking too much to expect all the people to decide. The danger inherent in extreme popular democracy is suggested by the title of one of Kipling's short stories, "The Town That Voted the Earth Was Flat."

Representative government is called for because of the demands of present-day societies. In foreign policy particularly, as John Jay recognized in *Federalist* No. 64, "perfect secrecy and immediate dispatch are sometimes requisite." As for the Congress, Alexander Hamilton wrote in *Federalist* No. 75, "Decision, secrecy, and dispatch, are incompatible with the genius of a body so variable and numerous." The need for dispatch demonstrates the place once again of the balancing truth. Presidential leadership indeed requires patiently guiding a whole society but it also demands seizing the moment. A philosophy of governance which hides the dual nature of executive leadership serves neither democracy nor the people—whatever the short-run political gains. A legislative assembly, Lippmann wrote, cannot negotiate with other governments; only the executive or his representative can do this and to pander to the public in political campaigns by promising complete openness and then to employ secret diplomacy in practice can only weaken the fragile fabric of trust and understanding between the executive and the people. Then, in the founders' words: "Without trust the republic perishes."

The president must make himself credible to the people, must help them to understand the philosophy of governance from which he proceeds, and the principles he employs in deciding on specifics. It is not enough for him to be energetic or well-informed "on every issue under the sun"; nor does his leadership end with recasting institutional or organizational patterns. His job is not done when he adds or subtracts from his staff. A larger view of relationships will always be needed. Values compete and conflict with one another. The people will not be deceived by talk of an easy harmony of interests between group and group, value and value. In politics as in personal life, responsibility entails tragic choices and to obscure this reality is to plant seeds of disillusionment and despair. The founders did not shrink from drawing up hierarchies of values and interests; nor can any current president who would retain the public trust. If presidential studies begin with concepts and organization, they end with the public philosophy.

5

Governmental Institutions Reconsidered: Public Enemy or the People's Servant

If history has confirmed some prophecies and refuted others, those which head the list of bright and shining visions repudiated by history involve the quest for public happiness. The Declaration of Independence singled out "the pursuit of happiness" as the best hope of individual satisfaction for a newly independent people. "To secure these rights, governments are instituted among men" and Thomas Jefferson and the other signers of the Declaration assumed that government by the consent of the governed would enhance and foster human happiness. Jefferson, who composed his draft of the Declaration in seventeen days between June 11 and June 28, 1776, intended his statement to be an expression of the American mind. He believed that by placing before mankind the common sense of the American claim to independence and its consequences, he would justify to the world the cause of freedom. His biographer, Virginia's Dumas Malone, tells us that Jefferson consulted no book or pamphlet; nor had he any compelling desire to be original. John Adams and Benjamin Franklin introduced certain minor changes into the draft. Congress vigorously debated the final document for three days from July 2 to July 4 with critics opposing phrases and whole statements, but with John Adams defending every word in Jefferson's draft. Franklin in its defense told an amusing story of a hatter whose inscription for a handsome signboard met such hostile criticism that all that remained on the signboard was his name and the picture of a hat. Notwithstanding Jefferson's defenders, his critics made changes, some for the better, but the famed philosophical passage which contained Jefferson's

summary of human rights and a justification of revolution survived as the most enduring portion of the entire document. Congress made official Jefferson's words, including his phrase on "the
pursuit of happiness."

Historians have noted that Jefferson, who in other respects followed John Locke, substituted for Locke's use of the sacred right
of property as integral to the fate of democracy the phrase "the
pursuit of happiness." Jefferson's contemporaries in all likelihood
did not see in the phrase a radical departure from Locke. As
Dumas Malone has written: "Locke presupposed the pursuit of
happiness, and Jefferson always assumed as basic the right of an
individual to hold property." Yet Jefferson's substitution was probably deliberate and "if it does not clearly indicate a philosophical
distinction between different sorts of rights it does suggest the
characteristic shading of his thought."[1] There can be little doubt,
judging by Jefferson's later actions and statements, that he placed
individual rights such as freedom of conscience and belief above
all other rights. Property like government was for Jefferson essential not as an end in itself but as a means to human happiness.
Jefferson quite possibly did not recognize the full implications of
his doctrine. He was a rather fastidious gentleman and a private
person who disliked the masses and their behavior. He brought
conviction rather than sentimentality to his writing. As he declared
in 1801 in his inaugural address: "I know, indeed, that some honest
men fear that a republican government cannot be strong—that this
government is not strong enough. I believe this, on the contrary,
the strongest government on earth. I believe it is the only one
where every man, at the call of law, would fly to the standard of
the law, and would meet invasions of the public order as his own
private concern."

When the twelve states agreed on July 4, 1776, to the written
Declaration, with the delegates from New York not voting, the
main common bond that united them was the goal of independence. The crowds which assembled on the Common in Philadelphia
did not call Jefferson forward to be honored as its author. The
fame of the Declaration and its historic affirmations lay in the
future. It was the event of breaking the ties with England, how-

ever, not the statement of a democratic philosophy of government that evoked wide popular response. It remained for Abraham Lincoln more than a generation later to signal the full importance of Jefferson's philosophy, saying:

> "All honor to Jefferson—to the man, who in the concrete pressure of a struggle for national independence by a single people, had the coolness, forecaste [*sic*], and sagacity to introduce into a merely revolutionary document an abstract truth, applicable to all men and all times, and so to embalm it there that today and in all coming days it shall be a rebuke and a stumbling-block to the very harbingers of reappearing tyranny and oppression."[2]

Jefferson's underlying faith in human nature, in man's indestructible will to carve out his own destiny in union with his fellow men and, therefore, in the essential truths of democracy is both refreshing and a little old-fashioned for much of contemporary discourse. The critics of democracy have challenged his philosophy in general and its relevance as applied to particular societies and cultures. Democracy seems ill-adapted to the needs of today's newly independent states, especially those who writhe in poverty and are unable to meet fundamental human needs. Third World leaders trumpet the call for alternative regimes better suited to mobilize scarce resources to provide food and housing for peoples ill-fed and helpless to protect themselves against the harsh inroads of virulent diseases and threatening natural and human enemies. Those opposing political ideologies that proclaim economic and social human rights enjoy immediate and short-run advantages in the contest between two divergent social and political philosophies. The struggle for the minds of men, moreover, goes on not at the level of high principle but on more primitive ground, that of sheer human survival. In the opening years of the 1980s, few would maintain that Jeffersonian democracy was everywhere on the march; hungry people are more likely to turn to political and economic creeds which offer shortcuts to human happiness.

Even within the notably successful democracies, the debate over democratic rights is confounded by the urgencies of the moment.

The United States is no exception. In one sense, the intellectual
and political controversy which has always surrounded democracy
is never divorced from economic and social realities. For the masses
and indeed for many signers of the Declaration of Independence,
freedom from Britain was a more compelling cause than fundamental human rights. Decades later, Alexis de Tocqueville was to
ask why the Americans "are so restless in the midst of their prosperity." He was baffled by the paradoxical fact that freedom and
prosperity had not produced happiness and he observed: "In
America I saw the freest and most enlightened men placed in the
happiest circumstances that the world affords; it seemed to me as
if a cloud habitually hung upon their brow, and I thought them
serious and almost sad, in their pleasures."[3]

The reason as de Tocqueville identified it was that Americans
were forever brooding over advantages they did not possess. He
wrote: "It is strange to see with what feverish ardor the Americans
pursue their own welfare, and to watch the vague dread that con-
stantly torments them lest they should not have chosen the shortest
path which may lead to it."[4] The inhabitants of the United States
cling to material goods as if they would live forever. They clutch
everything but hold fast to nothing because they shift their attention to any new object promising fresh gratification. A profound
restlessness sweeps across the land. Men build houses for their old
age but sell them before their construction is completed; they
embrace one profession but exchange it for another. They use their
leisure not for self-improvement but to travel the length and
breadth of the land. History to be sure offers countless examples of
persons in other cultures who spent their energies in the unending
pursuit of changing interests but seldom an instance of a whole
people so engaged.

The roots of the nation's disquietude were to be found for de
Tocqueville in the interplay of materialism and equality. He who
sets his heart exclusively upon the pursuit of wordly welfare ultimately yields to anxiety, fear, and regret because he finds little
satisfaction in the paths he follows to happiness. Equality as the
highest social principle guiding the individual's course accentuates
his restlessness and disillusionment. He conceives lofty aims which

confront stubborn obstacles to their attainment. A sense of frustration and powerlessness overcomes him. "When men are nearly alike and all follow the same track, it is very difficult for any one individual to walk quickly and cleave a way through the dense throng." The gulf between the promises of equality and their attainment makes for discontent, not happiness. However tireless such men may be in seeking equality, "the inequality of minds . . . still remain, which, coming directly from the hand of God, will forever escape the laws of man." In societies which respect inequality, it is possible to be happy in a lowly station of life; in a regime of equality men never attain all that they desire. They catch a glimpse of their goal but it escapes them. "To these causes must be attributed that strange melancholy which . . . haunts the inhabitants of democratic countries in the midst of their abundance, and that disgust at life which sometimes seizes upon them in the midst of calm and easy circumstances."[5]

THE TRIVIALIZATION AND MAGNIFICATION OF PUBLIC LIFE

Two centuries have passed since the Declaration of Independence and over a century since de Tocqueville wrote his great work. Americans anxious about man's condition and the future of the republic ask how enduring are the truths enshrined in Jefferson's public philosophy and in de Tocqueville's observations. Given society's profound scientific changes and the decades separating the past and present, the question inescapably poses itself to what extent can philosophers from another age speak to present needs. Today's urgent problems—inflation, environmental deterioration, and the decline of the cities—were not burning concerns for Jefferson and de Tocqueville, although Jefferson warned of the high costs of urbanization for a democracy. At another level, however, de Tocqueville's impressions of deep-seated public dissatisfaction and a condition of melancholy are more visible than ever before. Americans are more restless in the midst of abundance than at any other time in history. Modern man, who according to Robert J. Lifton is in "constant need of a meaningful inner formulation of self and [of the] world in which his own actions, and even impulses, have some kind of 'fit' with the 'outside' as he perceives it," seeks in vain for such formulations.[6] Man's life is pervaded by a "profound inner sense of absurdity." The connection between beliefs and events has been torn asunder and the individual cast adrift on troubled and uncertain seas. The prevailing condition of man is "spiritual homelessness." Idealists join realists in warning of the consequences of the crisis in values. In Rollo May's words: "People . . . have lost . . . the inner capacity to *affirm*, to experience values and goals as real and powerful for them."[7] The result, according to May, is that elements of the self are continually experimented with and as readily altered, and new idea systems and ideologies are embraced, modified, let go, and reembraced. Man's anxious and restless pursuit of new experiences has been transfered to experiments involved in the search for identity and self. Modern society has lost for most people its anchors of thought.

In part, the cause of such despair and malaise is remediable. The culture has lost its sense of history and its ability to measure itself against examples from living history, not against impossible dreams. The nation's attainment of life, liberty, and the pursuit of happiness is judged against an ideal norm, not against the annals of history. Because America is so rich and so powerful, its children praise or condemn its institutions and public life by standards that problably exceed the reach of man. If society had a better grasp of comparative history, it would evaluate its relative successes and failures against the background of the story of liberty and the pursuit of happiness in ancient Greece or Rome, Imperial Britain, or Soviet Russia. Unless a people have known the denial of freedom, how are they to appreciate its blessings? When all standards are drawn from "beyond history," the small incremental gains painfully wrought over time are ignored for want of historical comparisons. Not by accident, a generation with less sense of history—the generation of the late 1960s—judged society more harshly than any previous generation.

At the same time, other aspects of the present malaise and anxiety have deeper, less remediable causes. Jefferson was a child of the Enlightenment, wedded, albeit with healthy skepticism, to the theory of progress. Looking forward to the diffusion of knowledge and the establishment of fundamental human rights, he envisaged a political system "by which every fibre could be eradicated of ancient or future aristocracy." He was a crusader against ignorance and reminded his countrymen that "if a nation expects to be ignorant and free . . . it expects what never was and never will be." Ten days before his death, Jefferson wrote of the symbol for the world of the Fourth of July in words characteristic of his undying faith in man's progress:

> May it be to the world, what I believe it will be (to some parts sooner, to other later, but finally to all), the signal . . . to burst the chains under which monkish ignorance and superstition had persuaded them to bind themselves, and to secure the blessings and security of self-government. That form . . . restores the free right to the unbounded exercise of reason and freedom of opinion. . . . The general spread of the light of science has already laid open to every view the palpable truth, that the mass of mankind has not been born with saddles on their backs, nor a favored few, booted and spurred, ready to ride them legitimately for the Grace of God.[8]

It is obvious that the spread of science, which for Jefferson was to end "monkish ignorance and superstition" has brought untold benefits. Its application has provided societies and governments with resources for achieving a better world. Yet governments today, despite all these advances and more, enjoy less public confidence than in Jefferson's day. Public opinion polls report not only the loss of trust in public but in private institutions. The Fourth of July can scarcely be said to constitute "a signal to men everywhere to burst their chains." Free-booted tyrants may be less evident within the boundaries of democratic states but the claim is less frequently heard that tyranny is dead in the world. Even within the democracies, new forms of tyranny spring up including what de Tocqueville feared most, the tyranny of the majority.

Nor is dissatisfaction confined to man's relation to the state. A recent poll revealed that 60 percent of American workers were unhappy in their jobs. Moreover, their frustration and boredom was such that 36 percent were in search of other employment. If one seeks an explanation for their unhappiness, de Tocqueville's century-old description of American "restlessness in abundance" provides a starting point. American national character and the compulsions of equality clearly have something to do with present-day unrest. In societies in which inequality is taken for granted, the restless quest by everyone for something better is conspicuously absent. In cultures such as ours, men assume that if society is functioning as it should, there need be no permanent obstacles to the individual's advancement. Yet the phenomenon de Tocqueville identified has in our time been raised to a new level. In a society supposedly prospering from all science's inventions, individual and group dissatisfaction have increased to unprecedented proportions. The universal diffusion of the blessings of science and learning has curiously enough accentuated man's unrest. Incumbent presidents speak increasingly of a national malaise. The instruments of public information which in the Jefferson heritage were looked to as vehicles of popular enlightment are seen by American statesmen and commentators as part of the problem.

Partisan criticism aside, and allowing for the defensiveness of beleaguered political leaders who feel betrayed by the mass media, the question must be asked what is the role of the media in producing dissatisfaction and distrust. This question is one which has been raised by the nation's most responsible newsmen. It is suggested by the assertion of a leading television executive that the media have in practice become the political process, crowding out older practices of rallying the electorate. If it is true that the influence of the media is all-pervasive, that the medium has become the message, and that television's blitz campaigns at the height of national elections have supplanted traditional electioneering, it will not do for media executives to hide behind the easy explanation that the media merely reports the news and that they are a neutral force in society.

The indictment which those who would defend the media and public information and education agencies must overturn is that they bear responsibility, paradoxically enough, both for the trivialization and magnification of public life. The case against the media for the trivialization of public life rests on the public testimony of insiders no less than outsiders, of men such as the respected CBS anchorman Walter Cronkite as well as television and social critics.

Nielsen ratings and television technology have combined to push programmers to emphasize quantity over quality, sensationalism over straightforward reporting, the dramatic event over unfolding history, and the simple over the complex. News events are encapsulated in sixty-second packages of reporting. Despite repeated requests from newsmen like Cronkite that they be granted sixty rather than thirty minutes to report the news, the only sixty-minute program is a popular CBS report of that name which is part exposé, part entertainment, and part hard-line reporting laying bare wrong-doing and social irresponsibility at home and abroad. Whatever its strengths in generating public interest and controversy, "Sixty-Minutes" is hardly designed to build attitudes of public trust. Gone from major network programming are the nightly five-to-seven-minute background radio commentaries for which Edward R. Murrow, Elmer Davis, and Raymond Gram Swing became famous. Gone too are the regularly scheduled CBS Reports produced by Murrow and Fred Friendly and the end-of-the-year in-depth roundups of CBS reporters around the world. Those who seek public enlightenment on complex social and political issues must find it off prime time on such network discussion programs as "Agronsky and Company" and such educational television productions as "Washington Week in Review" and, at a more philosophical level, "Bill Moyers' Journal."

One by one, the last of the television commentators, including Eric Sevareid and Howard K. Smith, have been banished from the air whether by reason of age or network policy. Yet the social forces which make the news are not isolated events which occasion public controversy but the deeper tides of history. It is at this point that the media have failed society and left the average citizen baffled and bewildered by the kaleidoscopic reporting of isolated events. At a more parochial level, scholars and students of public affairs have reason for complaints. Recently, a reporter called on me to request an interview preparatory to writing an article for a regional magazine. What could I tell him about controversies in which my public affairs center was engaged, he asked, explaining that his editor had counseled him that only an account which could generate dissension would have enough public interest

to merit publication. Patient and serious scholarship on vital national issues evidently fell outside the boundaries of "news fit to
print."

However, the major sources of the trivialization of the news lie
deeper than media programming and technology. They strike at
the rational foundations of democracy itself. When Jefferson wrote
of the beneficent effects of the spread of science and reason, he
envisaged a serious dialogue that the media apparently rejects. As
his major writings and selected correspondence reveal, he considered that measured discussion of all the great issues of constitutional government was an appropriate subject for public discourse; he devoted his energies to private correspondence with
simple people no less than to that with Adams and Franklin. His
private papers show that he labored as diligently to express himself clearly to a young woman who had asked his views concerning
the health-giving properties of the waters of certain mineral springs,
as to clarify his stand on the issue of slavery to constituents and
fellow statesmen. The impoverishment of media discussions on
modern-day issues like slavery is illustrated in the predominance
of exposés, accounts of fraud and deception and of wrongdoing in
the field of public health and every other sphere.

More fundamental still, the focus of much present-day reporting
is on the so-called human side of the news. Public reporting seems
designed to cut public figures down to size. Much of public business is nothing less than hard slogging and patient trial and error
to bring a problem under control. Characteristically, it entails a
bargaining process that seeks to reconcile apparently divergent interests. When advances are made in public policy each side gives
a little to gain a part of its major goal or objective. Yet compromise in public life has a negative coloration; it smacks of horse
trades and of smoke-filled rooms. However, compromise is the
cement that holds together groups with conflicting interests and
makes possible the continued workings of the democratic political
process. When compromise and give and take break down, politics
yields to open conflict—to legislative impasse, civil violence, and
industrial strikes domestically and war internationally. Yet public
information systems are such that bold and heroic statements of

goals and intentions which are in conflict with other opposing goals and intentions make front-page news, not conflict resolution or the politics that Woodrow Wilson defined as the "slow boring of hard wood."

It is paradoxically the case that the selfsame authors of bold public statements who receive broad network coverage are assumed to be men of clay. Since everyone is equal, no leader is any better or any worse than any other public figure. All work under the shadow of some form of presumed guilt. For some, the process involved in the dismantling of public stature takes longer than others. Those who are telogenic, who appeal to prevailing concepts or stereotypes of the model leader, may for longer or shorter periods escape the devastating effects of relentless public disclosure. Sooner or later, though, their human frailty, local eccentricities, or group identification tarnish and deface their public image. As the media has the power to create a public personality, it equally has the power to destroy that image.

The trivialization of public life proceeds on many other levels. A recent book by Congressman Paul Findley deals with Lincoln's two-year term as a representative from the Seventh congressional district of Illinois.[9] Findley in an admirable study traces Lincoln's career in Congress, his struggle with the early issues of slavery, his protests against the war against Mexico, and his emergence as a major political figure on the national scene in the 1850s. Yet even Findley, in the spirit of the times, cannot forbear disclosing that Lincoln allegedly padded his expense accounts and charged the taxpayers more for his trips between Springfield and Washington than he actually spent. It may be true as Edmund Wilson wrote in *Patriotic Gore: The Studies in the Literature of the American Civil War* that "there has undoubtedly been written about Abraham Lincoln more romantic and sentimental rubbish than about any other American figure." To turn from sentimentalism to triviality, however, hardly seems to advance human understanding.

The litany of trivialization of past and present chief executives has become all too familiar. In spite of the fact that the society flaunts its advance beyond puritanism and prudishness on sexual questions, a president's extramarital adventures, whether real or imaginary, head the list. No surviving heir or part-time secretary is immune from interrogation by writers or news-gatherers. We are told more about the sexual life of Franklin D. Roosevelt, Dwight D. Eisenhower, John F. Kennedy, Henry Kissinger, and Gerald Ford than about neglected chapters in their political history. No aspect of family life or the trials and tribulations of their children's advance through adolescence is ignored. The public is informed in exquisite detail about presidential illnesses, private conversations and personal relations, about whether or not a president reads in the bathroom, his bedroom conversations with his wife, his daily exercise, his battle with fish or rabbits or both during private fishing trips, and his relationship with favorite or less favorite sons, parents, brothers, sisters, cousins, or aunts. No one would question that some and perhaps all of such personal matters can illuminate the character of a leader. What trivializes these subjects, however, is the spirit in which they are investigated and disclosed and the unrelenting zeal of the media in pursuit of exposés. If questions of personal and social relations were related directly to the president's performance and his ability to conduct his public responsibilities, the charge of trivialization would carry little weight. In his classic work on Napoleon, the British historian Herbert Butterfield wrote:

> He was a military leader and we see him organising armies, calling up recruits, disposing his forces, ordering shoes for his soldiers, arranging the construction of bakeries, busying himself with all the paraphernalia of war. He was a human mortal, and we hear of him enjoying the balls and the brilliant life of Warsaw, adoring the beauty of the Polish ladies, laying siege to the heart of the Countess Walewska, and writing to the Empress to reassure her about his health, or to calm her jealousies or to prevent her from appearing inconveniently in Poland. He was the Emperor, ruling France from a distance, organizing propaganda, directing theatres and newspapers, rebuking his chief of police, aiding necessitous manufactures in France, and writing "M. de Champagny, literature ought to be encouraged."[10]

Butterfield sought to clarify the integral relation between Napoleon's historic role as an imperial leader, his conquests and farflung military campaigns, and his affection for an attractive woman who was not his wife. Butterfield's allusion to Countess Walewska and his handling of that relationship helps us to perceive a dimension of Napoleon's personality and character affecting his leadership. By comparison, observers note in the exposés of recent presidents a mean-spirited attitude, a certain mischievousness and a pandering to the lust of the masses. The major purpose of such revelations seems to be to sell newspapers and television advertising. They represent an appeal to the lowest impulses of men and have the effect both of damaging personal reputations and weakening respect for the public interest. They put private performance far above public capacity in leadership assessment. One might have expected more of the inheritors of Jefferson's tradition of reason and science.

If the resources for a more enlightened approach to public affairs were not present, the questioning of the trivialization of public life would not stand scrutiny. Not only are the technical means at hand, however, but the nation's intellectual resources are abundant. Technically, the media's capacity for bringing its viewers onto the field of action is breathtaking in performance. Not only athletic contests but symphonies and Shakespeare, state funerals and meetings of heads of state, inaugural ceremonies and political assassinations, and missile launches and walks on the moon are brought into "everyman's" living room. The words of a periodic radio and television program of the 1940s, "You Were There," have been translated into regular television fare lacking only the informing explanation of commentaries by an Edward R. Murrow. Indeed the most conspicuous weaknesses of media reporting cluster together in what might be called political and social interpretation. The media's greatest social achievements are in portraying the "what" of contemporary history: what happened when and where. Its conspicuous failures relate to the "why" of political events. The media in its analysis does best with palpable factors: hardware and throw-weight, velocity and cruise radius, megatons and force ratios. Its finest hours may quite possibly have been Walter Cronkite's reporting of the triumphs and tragedies of the space program including the moon walk. With all the hazards and uncertainties of

the space age, scientists have programmed with extraordinary
precision the flight of space vehicles from point to point, from
launch-pad to reentry; commentators like Cronkite in turn have
transmitted and explained the process to millions of listeners. It
is difficult to think of a parallel in the political realm to match the
clarity and comprehension of such historic landmarks in media
reporting.

The search for explanations of this disparity brings us back to
the differences between scientific and political reality. Scientific
explanations rest on quantitative and measurable factors. The sum
total of reality yields to a reductionist approach; variables are
considered in relationship to fixed and widely accepted scientific
principles. Social and political reality is composed of a multitude
of independent variables with little consensus on the methods for
interpreting and explaining them. For instance, foreign policy
analysis depends upon a host of unknowns: alien cultures, novel
political and constitutional arrangements, untried leaders, and the
accidents of political and military history. Even here, the analysis
of a handful of exceptional interpreters has stood the test of time.
As with political leadership, competence in political reporting is
more art than science. Unique forces intrude on recurrent practice. Much of political analysis proceeds, as does wise decision
making, on the basis of instincts and hunches or what the Indonesian philosopher Soedjatmoko has called blind groping. It is
expecting too much to ask that reporters perform the role of political analysts, but much of media reporting on foreign affairs is
amateurish, lacking in sound political reasoning and devoid of
wisdom and judgment. Given the constraints of the media and the
frantic pursuit of ratings, it is difficult to imagine media executives
turning to analysts of the quality of Lippmann or Churchill. In
consequence, the hard-pressed citizen, shaken and bewildered by a
barrage of seemingly unrelated political facts, becomes of necessity
his own political analyst. Everyman's view of politics and foreign
policy becomes as trustworthy as anyone else's views. The myth of
equality reinforces the impulse of every American to be his own
expert.

Furthermore, another force is at work substituting for analysis the cherished respect men show for numbers and statistics. The columnist Meg Greenfield writes that Americans "are the most weighed, counted, measured . . . society in the history of civilization." She argues "that most of our political figures concern who gets to do the weighing and counting (Keeper of the Data is our Keeper of the Flame), and that as a consequence . . . we have begun to talk about ourselves as if we were someone else." Things are always different than they appear. "Are you feeling strapped? How odd—the data show that you have never been better off and are the justifiable envy of the world. Are you in a pretty good mood despite your financial tight place? Like hell you are—you're on a real emotional and spiritual downer and we've got the charts and equations to prove it." The data are the final arbiter. "There is always a study someplace, a graph, a survey . . . a poll, an equation that suggests . . . that the unemployed are working, the working are unemployed and that there is 8.7 percent more air pollution in Antarctica than there is on the Los Angeles freeway." The problem with numbers, Ms. Greenfield asserts, is that "great numbers of the number people don't know what they are talking about." The ordinary American lives in a split-screen world. "There are two realities simultaneously playing themselves out before our eyes: the way we feel and the way we are told the data show we feel." Because we are an insecure·society, because we doubt our own impressions and because the media provides little guidance, we await the next set of tests and soundings. Without them: "How can you tell whether you like Jimmy Carter or your child is getting anything worth knowing at school or hamburger costs more than you can pay or things are better or worse than before?"[11] Greenfield stops short of asking the question "What would history have been like if Churchill had waited for the latest opinion poll to decide on the defense of Britain?" How would the story have come out if the Grand Alliance had been forged against Hitler on the strength of the latest data? How would Lincoln have decided on raising an army for preserving the Union if the prerequisite had been attitude testing through survey research? For the great crisis issues of public policy, statistical data partake of the same quality of triviality as media reports of the president's reading habits or of his struggle with a rabbit. The anxious pursuit of the latest fragment of statistical data about what the public thinks when it may not be thinking at all makes of the statesman a robot bobbing helplessly on an ocean of numbers.

The other side of the dilemma of contemporary public life is a product of its magnification. Every facet of the political process, and especially presidential politics, is assumed to be the public's business. Whenever an administration has tried to hold to itself some aspect of the task of resolving the collective will, a rival political group has promised a more open administration. The consequences of such promises have been twofold: first, after a longer or shorter interval of ostensibly open government, the new administration has predictably retreated to private policy making and diplomacy, as the Carter administration was forced to do in its summit diplomacy at Camp David. Second, expansive talk of a wholly open approach to the difficult tasks of governance has spread confusion and led to abuses both by the rulers and the media which have had disastrous consequences. Leaders, and once again particularly the president, have been expected to have answers to every problem. (Henry Kissinger wryly observed that one of his successors had more solutions than there were problems and, in more earthy language, Bert Lance proclaimed, "If it ain't broke, don't fix it.") Leaders who pride themselves on openness not only seek to have answers for every question but speak publicly off the cuff without time for reflection on highly sensitive and volatile issues. Every thought and response of a chief executive becomes potentially a headline event. The media rush in to capitalize on the ill-advised comments and improvisations of the nation's principal leader placing him at the center of public controversy and debate.

The magnification of public life misleads the public to expect answers before policies have taken shape. They cast the president in the role of chief administrator called on to answer questions and resolve disputes more appropriately the responsibility of heads of departments. If he yields to the temptation to speak and act on every issue, he prepares the way for national distrust and disillusionment. It is heady wine for the leader to believe the image makers and media moguls who magnify every detail of presidential thought and action. Confronted with the media's determination to make of the president a miracle man and omniscient authority on every twist and turn in the totality of the political process, the skillful president spars and parries with his interrogators while the ignorant leader speaks when he should be silent.

The result is loss of dignity for the president, the decline of public respect, the dissolution of trust, and an erosion of faith in his capacity to lead. The mystique of leadership requires the need for both resolve and restraint. Indecision may be a weakness but so are thoughtlessness and words that are not measured against their possible consequences. The president is of the people, the one elected official chosen by the nation at large. If he would remain in his high office, he can never afford to lose touch with the people. At the same time, he must, if he would preserve his office's legitimacy, stand above every partisan struggle, and be an example to the people, not a reflection of their whims and caprice. He is more than the public writ large; he has responsibilities they do not carry. To magnify every fashion and foible of the people and to mirror their habits and fancies may afford him certain passing strengths as a politician. They will not make him a respected leader. In the final analysis, he must in a certain sense be from but not of the people. A president must be more than the public's Charley McCarthy. There must be both a public and a private side to his leadership. Since he cannot be all things to all men, he must reserve to himself some of the dignity and inherited symbols of office. Henry Clay said of policies the nation had no thought of defending, "There is no dignity in them." As the president must resist the trivialization of public life, he must also oppose its magnification.

THE GOVERNMENT AS ENEMY OR SERVANT

In the minds of the founding fathers of the Republic, establishment of a federal government was conceived as a high moral and political end. George Washington in his letter transmitting the Constitution to the Congress wrote: "In all our deliberations . . . we kept steadily in our view, that which appears to us the greatest interest of every true American, the consolidation of our Union, in which is involved our prosperity, felicity, safety, perhaps our national existence." He paid tribute to "the spirit of amity" and "mutual deference" which the "political situation rendered indispensable." He acknowledged the difficulty of drawing up with precision those rights which had to be surrendered by individuals and the thirteen states and those which were reserved to them. He made no attempt to conceal regional and state differences arising from divergent interests and circumstances and which decreed that in creating a government the full "approbation of every State is not . . . to be expected." Yet "each will . . . consider, that had her interest alone been consulted, the consequences might have been particularly disagreeable or injurious to others." What united different interests and states was the common hope and belief that a federal government would "promote the lasting welfare of . . . [the] country . . . and secure her freedom and happiness."[12]

Government to secure freedom and happiness was to be the servant of the people, not their master, and the founders were determined that so fundamental an objective not be left to chance. The author of *Federalist* No. 51 (presumably Madison) found that government was the "greatest of all reflections on human nature. . . . In framing a government which is to be administered by men over men, the great difficulty lies in this: you must first enable the government to control the governed; and in the next place to control itself." One restraint which is no doubt the primary control is the will of the people but "experience has taught mankind the necessity of auxiliary precautions." Therefore power must be used to check power and ambition to counteract ambition. Each department of government must be assigned the constitutional means to resist encroachment by others. While men often proceed on the basis of noble intentions, they also act from baser motives. The need to supply checks and balances may be seen throughout human affairs, private as well as public. In government, the private interest of every individual is a sentinel over public rights. Government must be so constructed that "its several constituent parts may, by their mutual relations, be the means of keeping each other in their proper places."[13]

Government, then, was so organized that a just distribution of power within the political system would safeguard the rights of individuals and groups. Federalism would "preserve the constitutional equilibrium between the general and the State governments." At the same time, its mission, novel in the world, was to "vindicate the honor of the human race" and teach moderation. Public confidence in government as the founders conceived it would result from its ability to provide for public safety and the common defense. It would respond to public wants through the general power of taxation accorded it by which its resources are kept equal to its necessities. An energetic government was essential to security against external and internal dangers; a stable government was "essential to national government and . . . to that repose and confidence in the minds of the people, which are among the chief blessings of civil society."[14] The genius of liberty demanded that government be kept close to the people and that public servants should enjoy appointments of short duration, whereas stability demanded a certain continuity for those who govern. Thus liberty and stability had to be kept in balance.

In this, as in all other matters, the public interest must be controlling. A republican government is one which derives its just power from the consent of the governed, and however widely the term *republic* is applied, the element of consent, directly or indirectly derived, is its essential feature. Consent must come not from a favored class but from the great body of the people. Ultimately, the Constitution must be judged, wrote Madison in its defense, by whether or not it contributes to public happiness and the public trust. The founders called on the people to accept the Constitution because it represented, not a perfect system, but "the best that the present . . . circumstances . . . permit." They had recourse to the words of David Hume in defending the new government: "To balance a large state . . . is a work of so great difficulty, that no human genius . . . is able, by the mere dint of reason and reflection, to effect it. The judgment of many must unite in the work; experience must guide their labor; time must bring it to perfection, and the feeling of inconveniences must correct the mistakes which they inevitably fall into in their first trials and tribulations."[15] Drawing on Hume, the founders placed their trust on the possibility of change, warning against anarchy, alienation, and civil strife if commitments were not made to an admittedly imperfect government. However worthy the new government, its future demanded experience, moderation, and political fortitude. They saw in a government based on the voluntary consent of a whole people a prodigious attainment and in its downfall nothing less than an awful spectacle. Prudence demanded its defense and support.

It may be helpful for contemporary Americans to recall that not everyone rallied to the support of the Constitution (the founders spoke of the precarious support of only seven of the thirteen states). We may be comforted in our present disunity by divisions which were present "at the creation." Even then, in circumstances as perilous as the Republic has known, what came to be known as the working majority of government was frequently in doubt. Less in doubt were the elements of a public philosophy crafted by minds richly endowed who sought to define with clarity and elegance first principles of responsible government. The beginnings of the rediscovery of an idea of government around which a divided public can rally was undertaken directly by the nation's civil and political leaders. It was not assigned to a coterie of well-paid speech writers or left to a national commission.

If the government today is viewed as the people's enemy, one cause may be the divorce of thought and action. If the energies of leaders are consumed in political maneuvering, leaving the definition and description of this to men who, as one former presidential speech writer put it, see the primary purpose of their rhetoric as "kicking the opposition in the stomach," is it any wonder that political life has deteriorated? What is true of public life is equally true of private life, as hard-hitting speech writers shuttle back and forth between service to presidents and the chief executives of oil companies and media networks, who themselves have come under fire. What could be more unrealistic than to expect political fire fighters with little direct experience in government and less knowledge of political philosophy to match Hamilton or Jefferson or Madison? The fault is not theirs, for they have become the literary mercenaries of our age much as the nations of Europe drew soldier-mercenaries from countries such as Switzerland in another age. They wield their pens as Swiss mercenaries carried guns in the service of warring political factions. Yet neither group could possess the wisdom to map out larger strategies of war and peace. No Swiss mercenary supposed he had the knowledge or the skill to substitute himself for Napoleon or Wellington in charting the course of military strategy. Yet modesty is a lost virtue for those present-day "word-merchants" who boldly assert, in private at least, that they determine the subject matter and timing as well as the substance of presidential speeches.

If America has lost its public philosophers who at the founding of the Republic helped set the nation on its course, it has also lost a substantial measure of its faith in a federal government which for Washington promised "prosperity, felicity, safety, . . . [and] national existence." We have less, it would seem, of that "spirit of amity" and "mutual deference" which "the political situation rendered indispensable." More serious, every special-interest group approaches its peculiar claim as though the Republic's survival depended on its immediate and total acceptance. We seem to have lost the sense that if only a single interest is consulted, the consequences can be "disagreeable or injurious to others." At the very moment every special-interest is calling for government to come to its aide and cities and industries are appealing to officials to bail them out; we appear to doubt that government is capable of promoting "the lasting welfare of . . . [the] country" and securing "her freedom and happiness."

Americans must ask themselves how it can be that we trusted government as a servant at the founding of the Republic and see it now as the enemy. One reason may be that whereas we earlier looked at government from the perspective of a philosophy of man and society, we approach it now as an instrument to do our selfish bidding. Each group defines its selfish interests as comprising the sole end of government. We each judge government by what it has done for us today. Because we find difficulty in restraining our own interests and claims, we also find it difficult to control government itself. No logical consistency exists between saying government

must be limited by checks and balances as the founders willed it
and calling on government to implement in unlimited ways of our
own narrow purposes and goals. By equating the attainment of
causes such as legislation on abortion or the instituting of wage-
price guidelines for others as against an unregulated economy for
my segment of industry with the survival and preservation of a
moral republic, we act as though we were angels and no government was necessary. We gouge one another, not from conscious
ambition and greed, understanding that the greed and ambition of
others will check and balance ours, but from some high moral
purpose. A philosophy of private interests, indeed many such philosophies, have been substituted for the public philosophy and the
idea of government as the servant of all stands in contradiction to
these exclusively self-centered philosophies. Government which had
been conceived as "the greatest of all reflections on human nature"
becomes the enemy of the champions of single-interest groups who
follow their selfish course and accept no restraints on their politics.

Nor have we kept alive the other lessons which were enshrined
in the writings of the founders. If it is primarily special interests
that government is expected to serve and if such interests are
zealously and self-righteously pursued, the need to proclaim moderation and restraint becomes self-evident. If the Republic's necessities are primarily my necessities, I come imperceptibly to question
the merits, for example, of the general powers of taxation. When a
group of people within society sees its cause as wholly just, it un-
derstands less fully the tension between itself and the whole and
between different objectives of government such as liberty and
stability. When doubts are spread about a government's ability to
provide for the common defense, it loses an element of national
prestige and its standing as a bulwark of freedom. Whenever some
group comes to question whether it has given its consent to policies the government is pursuing, the reputation of a state as resting
on the consent of the governed is damaged. If the people also
doubt that time will improve an imperfect government, another
dimension of public trust has been lost. If its downfall is no longer
viewed with alarm as an awful spectacle, the people's commitment
has lessened.

It should be clear from this broad-ranging sketch of the differences between the political values of the founders and those prevailing today that the road back to trust in government is through a rekindling of ancient political faiths. If it is said that this represents an impossible dream and that people and nations never retrace history, that argument is refuted by the founders themselves. They took their reference points from Greece and Rome, Europe and England. They saw past political experience as offering pointers by which to chart their political fortune, however novel their own constitutional inventions. If Americans for the 1980s would look back to the purposes of the founders, they can take as one precedent their forefathers' use of history. If there is a better way of rebuilding what has been lost—the view of the government as public servant—those who discover it should affirm it. Not hearing such affirmations, Americans would be wise to reexamine and rethink the thought of the founders.

6

Political Ideologies and Higher Values: Morality, Democracy, and Communism

Morality, democracy, and communism are large subjects, not ones that self-conscious social scientists or analytical philosophers normally address. We live in an era of specialization, each of us measuring and analyzing little fragments of reality, leaving the tides of history and the collision of world forces to political spokesmen and pundits. Yet leaders from the East and West and from the Third World are pressed, not with the latest versions of decision-making theories or global interdependence, but with questions of urgent human need, social justice, and the future of democracy and communism. Undergirding all discussions of these larger subjects are assumptions about right and wrong and morality in politics—a theme from which students of politics can apparently never escape.

The boundaries of a quest for a public philosophy are broader than democracy and communism; the idea of the public interest is not the monopoly of a single ideology or political system. Ideologies which offer prescriptions for the good life here and now are also reflections of more fundamental ideas of good and evil or right and wrong. Democracy which preserves and defends individual freedom is grounded in the idea of the sanctity of each human being. Communism, which emphasizes collective rights, has roots in traditions of social justice. Morality as expressed in the higher law or in principles of political philosophy is broader than any given political ideology. It provides standards by which ideologies can be measured and judged.

102

MORALITY

Discussions of morality and politics, and of international politics in particular, have suffered in the United States from two opposing viewpoints, moralism and cynicism. Moralism is the tendency to equate morality with a single moral end: the outlawry of war, collective security, and now human rights, to draw examples from the history of the last four decades. Utopianism and moralism have common intellectual and political roots. They not only separate out one single moral value but they make it an absolute to the exclusion of other values. To dramatize this outlook's narrow scope, one has only to ask "what human rights would survive a nuclear holocaust?" Moral reasoning requires that human rights in the 1980s and 1990s be related to other moral ends such as peace and the prevention of thermonuclear war.

Cynicism, by contrast, is the tendency to argue that morality is never linked or interconnected in any organic way with politics. Morality for this approach is nothing more than the justification, or ideological rationalization, for actions carried out for other reasons—"to make the worst appear the better cause." Morality is an impediment to progress, the opiate of the people, and a barrier thrown up to defend the weak and the powerless against the strong.

Yet in America these two viewpoints have never silenced discussion over what is right and wrong. Some of our leading moral, political, and legal philosophers have placed morality and politics at the center of their thought. As one reflects on their writings, one is impressed with the recurrence of five broad principles or general propositions:

1. Nations, like individuals, are never as moral as they claim to be. As the individual falls prey to moral pretentiousness (the parent who acts solely in the interest of his children), nations are swept along by powerful currents of national self-righteousness (my country, right or wrong). Nationalist crusades especially in the twentieth century become fanatical and cruel because "everyman"—the frustrated individual citizen personified by the lumpen proletariat in Nazi Germany—projects his own unrealized ambitions onto his nation's crusade for national supremacy.

2. Man is a moral being, as he is a social being, but is baffled by the question "what is right?" The complexities and ambiguities of present-day politics make moral choice extraordinarily difficult. Sometimes the most men can do, as suggested in Edmond Cahn's *The Sense of Injustice*, is to identify not justice but injustice. Determining what is right and just assumes men can foresee the consequences of political actions, yet history is strewn with the litter of failed prophecies. Who among the defenders of liberty, equality, and fraternity and of the French Revolution foresaw Napoleonic imperialism, or who anticipated that the Protestant Reformation would usher in the powerful European nation-state?

3. Morality in politics characteristically calls not for a choice between good and evil but for striking a balance between competing goods, between peace and justice, freedom and order, individual rights and national security. Not only is morality more than the choice of a single moral end, but each moral end, like crystal in the sunlight, is subject to change in the cross-lights of history. Politics imposes harsh choices, sometimes between lesser evils. Our greatest president, Abraham Lincoln, defined moral choice as identifying the plain physical facts, seeking to learn what was right and doing my best, in the hope history will bring me out all right.

4. Further, moral principles in politics are filtered through the circumstances of time and place, are shaped by historical necessities and are conditioned by the national interest. From the standpoint of personal morality, President Lincoln had no doubt that slavery was evil, yet he wrote Horace Greeley: "If I could save the Union without freeing *any* slaves I would do it, and if I could save it by freeing *all* the slaves I would do it; and if I could save it by freeing some and leaving others alone I would also do that. What I do about slavery, and the colored race, I do because I believe it helps to save the Union; and what I forbear, I forbear because I do *not* believe it would help to save the Union."[1]

5. Nevertheless, given the ambiguities of national and international politics, morality in politics demands that a tension be maintained between higher moral principles and the actualities of political practice. Men in politics who would be moral men must engage in an unending search for what is right and for policies and institutions that embody the right. We have forgotten, Paul

Freund tells us, the ancient tradition of moral reasoning and practical morality whose touchstone is seeking to reconcile what is morally right with what is politically possible. We have lost the ability to think creatively about the relationship of moral principles. "People are always extolling the man of principle," Oliver Wendell Holmes declared, "but . . . the superior man is the one who knows he must find his way in a maze of principles."

DEMOCRACY

The founding fathers held that democracy was grounded in certain concepts of human nature. The rights of man reside in the individual and government is denied authority to infringe on those rights. Democracy's defenders may be unduly modest in defending its creeds and its practice. Thus Winston Churchill explained: "Democracy is the worst system devised by the wit of man, except for all the others." An Asian, Jawaharlal Nehru, declared: "Democracy is good. I say this because other systems are worse." Perhaps the restraint verging on self-mockery of such democratic leaders was deliberately intended to hold down popular emotions, an achievement for which Cromwell is not remembered; for of him a contemporary wrote: "You shall scarce speak to . . . [him] about anything but he will lay his hand on his breast, elevate his eyes and call God to record. He will weep, howl and repent, even while he doth smite you under the fifth rib."

Democracy may be a more virtuous political system because it insists on holding the line taut between the recognition of moral principles and the acknowledgment that no individual or group can permanently preempt them. It provides viable structures within which men not once but continuously can seek to balance objective moral standards and political necessities. Antidemocratic thinkers despair of a system that gives changing content to moral principles within a pluralist political universe, but Niebuhr has challenged them, saying: "The fact that honest men see the hierarchy of moral values and principles in a different order according to their different perspectives must not discourage us from honestly seeking to do what is right. But it ought to dissuade us from all self-righteous assumptions that we alone are truly moral."

American democracy, therefore, has offered the world a fortuitous blending of, and a dual commitment to, moral principles and a pluralist political process. Those who deny that democracy rests on religious and moral foundations are as mistaken as those who would equate religion with politics. While the founders paid tribute to "the laws of nature and nature's God," they warned against established religion. Thomas Jefferson, while viewing religion as a personal and private matter, chose as his personal slogan Benjamin Franklin's motto: "Rebellion to tyrants is obedience to God." The hallmark of American democracy is its essential dualism: on one hand, a tradition of religious and moral beliefs closely linked with the higher law on which constitutionalism ultimately rests and, on the other, an independent, largely secularized political process which safeguards society against the sanctification of every practical political choice. Perhaps more than any other political philosophy, the democratic ideal seeks to preserve the separation of church and state while at the same time resisting their isolation. Jefferson and a long procession of American statesmen have been ambivalent about the connections between norms and realities. They recognized the laws of nature and nature's God mirrored in America's experiment of freedom. But they also maintained it was easier to discover and proclaim general principles in politics—especially in international politics—than to apply them in practice, as when they resisted declaring war against England in support of the ideals of the French Revolution.

A similar dualism has existed with respect to economic development, for although the Protestant ethic inspired Americans to strive for economic advancement and identified outward prosperity with inner virtue, Americans have always had an uneasy conscience about crass materialism. A nation which was the inheritor of two thousand years of slavery, disregard for women's rights, the countenancing of child labor, the abuse of prisoners, complacency about the poor or the ignorance of the masses has thrown off its shackles in the past fifty years. Equality of opportunity has crowded out slavery. Women are coming into their own. Prison reform has become a staple of legislatures and courts. Poverty, ignorance, and disease have become targets of national policy. For most Americans, poverty is no longer foreordained. Free and compulsory public education has been legislated. Health and well-being are at the center of the goals of a good society. In a relatively brief span of history, Americans have narrowed, though not eliminated, the gap between the is and the ought. And for our friends in the developing world who imagine that the United States has long been a land of abundance, it is worth recalling that in 1900, one out of five American infants died at birth (today the number is one out of forty); only one of a hundred homes had electric lights; the majority of Americans lived in rural areas; we had no system of social security or retirement benefits or health insurance, no pure food and drug acts, little public health, less sanitation, and too little social mobility and economic advancement.

It would be difficult to imagine so dramatic an advance taking place if there had not been an enduring tension between the moral foundations of democracy and the slow but irresistible workings of the democratic process. That same tension persists into the future and is making itself felt all along the line of democracy's unfinished agenda: the ravages of inflation, the decay of the cities, cutthroat competition, calculations of profit and loss eroding integrity, big government confounding civic virtue and public responsibility, the breakdown of standards in family life, the anonymity of urban life, and conflicts between narrow national self-interest and world responsibility.

Whatever its flaws, American democracy has provided the world with the example of an unfinished society in the process of becoming, and is meaningful for this reason to new states and old, to rich and poor in part because morality and politics are continuously in tension with one another. Moral principles stand outside democracy as a political ideology and provide standards by which its actions are judged.

COMMUNISM

In contrast with democracy, the rights of man under communism depend on the state and it is understood that the state will promote and facilitate those rights. Whereas the ultimate standards for democracy are external, they are internalized within communism as an ideology. Older Marxist theorists contend there are no rights apart from the state, although a handful of younger Marxist theorists privately maintain that rights are inherent in man's fundamental social relations, which the state must enhance and improve. Marxism's main contribution has been to throw the spotlight on the collective social order, as against Western liberalism's emphasis on individualism. Marxism has identified the perennial nature of group struggle but mistakenly assumed that all social conflict could be equated with the class struggle. Communism transmuted Marxist philosophy into a political religion under which every tactical and strategic move by communist regimes was justified and found its place in the dialectic of history. Thus Communist regimes which came to power promising to destroy the tyrannical political power of the privileged capitalist class have ended by drawing to themselves all economic and political power, as despised capitalists never succeeded in doing. In communism, morality has been made immanent or drawn inside the communist system.

For communism there is a single enemy—the bourgeoisie—and only one virtuous class, the proletariat. There is one overarching social need—to alter the means of production—and one paramount objective in foreign relations—to preserve communism in the hands of an ever more powerful state against capitalist encirclement. Social and economic rights take precedence in rhetoric and in some aspects of policy over political and civil rights. (Despite official rhetoric, Soviet society is suffering from shortages of food and medicine in rural areas and inadequate housing in the cities.) On all these points, communism resolves the dilemmas of political choice by following the dictates of utopianism and moralism—by subordinating all other moral and political ends to the achievement of the communist utopia. The current head of the Institute of Philosophy and Sociology in Moscow, when asked if communists still believed in the classless society and the withering away of the state, given present disparities in economic and social status, replied: Yes, of course, but twenty years may be required or perhaps another generation. Meantime, persecution continues, if not on the scale of Stalin's elimination of five million kulaks, but still justified by the nightmarish dream of a communist utopia.

Reinhold Niebuhr, perhaps the greatest of American theologians, periodically warned that moral perfectionists were lacking in prudence when they entered politics and were frequently ill-equipped to deal with the ambiguities of political and moral choice. The West's greatest student of diplomacy, Harold Nicolson, preferred the humane skeptic to the moralist in politics and diplomacy. Both recognized that such views placed them on the abyss of cynicism but they defended themselves, saying that they were saved by prudence and by preserving the tension between ultimate moral principles, never fully realizable, and proximate moral principles such as distributive justice. Robert Frost wrote that good fences make good neighbors. Even within man's most intimate community, the family, husband and wife or parents and children achieve a modicum of justice by drawing boundary lines within which they respect one another's most deeply held interests and convictions. Distributive justice is less than absolute justice and justice, defined as giving each man his due, falls short of love, which Niebuhr called the "impossible possibility." Yet justice informed by love and compassion is more likely to produce justice than those fixed and abstract doctrines which Paul Tillich found insufficient: "Morality is not slavish conformity to an unrelenting code." We observe something comparable in international politics, for most of the lasting agreements between East and West in the Cold War have resulted from tacit understandings, not formal legal arrangements which a public aroused by the strong tides of nationalism might have overturned. Compromise in politics, as the great British political philosopher Edmund Burke taught, contains elements of morality that are finally incorporated in some concept of distributive justice.

In the hard bargaining of international politics, the highest morality is often no more than the search for the points of convergence between sometimes conflicting, sometimes compatible national interests and ideals. Historically, this search has frequently occurred at the end of long periods of exhausting conflict and

war, but not because one or the other side had accepted the others'
ideals and values. In the sixteenth and seventeenth centuries, Protestants and Catholics stopped fighting one another because they
were war-weary, not because they had abandoned their religious
faiths. Cardinal Richelieu was as staunch a Catholic when he made
common cause with the Protestants in France and Holland as
when he fought the Protestants. Believers no less than cynics end
their struggles when they grow weary of conflict and conclude they
have more to gain from peace than war.

Accepting the fact that there are no perfect analogies in history, this ancient example may throw a small light on the present
crisis. Political theorists and public officials are lacking both in
professional vocabulary and personal modesty in describing the
present state of affairs. One side speaks of peaceful coexistence and
the other of detente and normalization, claiming more for the
scope and character of accommodation than has been achieved.
Yet looking back to the height of the Cold War in the late 1940s
and early 1950s, who would question that some measure of progress
has been made. In the late 1940s and early 1950s, Churchill, hardly
a friend of communism, repeatedly proclaimed: "Jaw, jaw is better
than war, war." President Eisenhower and Senators Walter George
and Richard Russell joined together to lay the groundwork for
what years later came to be called "the era of negotiations." Kennedy continued the tradition and, more forcefully than his predecessors and more modestly than his successors, expressed it in his
famed American University speech. Nixon was the first American
president to travel to Moscow and simultaneously to open up relations with China. The road to accommodation has been a difficult one marked from the beginning by more setbacks and detours
than advances, more obstacles than a smooth course, but the approach has unquestionably transformed the map of international
politics.

Yet "peaceful competition" must be accepted for what it is,
neither more nor less. The rivalry between East and West continues presently on the basis of substantial nuclear parity on a
global basis and within a multipolar world; it would be illusory
to suppose that the struggle is free of the gravest risks and dan-

gers. In this struggle, the Soviets are the true believers, yet anxious and troubled and fearful of steps that might threaten the dissolution of the Soviet empire. Americans are frank to acknowledge that the democracies have a broad agenda of unfinished business: the cities, the environment, inflation, and our minorities. In private, Soviet scholars and officials have been forthcoming in confessing mistakes and shortcomings but in public, dominated by their ideology, they present a united front reaffirming their well-known charges and creed; they remain unrelenting in their criticism of capitalist and neocolonialist America. Not only is criticism of the government prohibited, but for Marxists it is intellectually difficult to acknowledge error in policies and the dialectic of history for as Jean-Francois Revel, the controversial French socialist, writes: "Authoritarian socialism has failed almost everywhere, but you will not find a single Marxist who will say it has failed because it was wrong or impractical. He will say it has failed because nobody went far enough with it. So failure never proves that a myth is wrong." An exception is the disclosure of the crimes of past leaders, but as Revel explains, "Communist historians describe Stalin's crimes—in the open-minded moments when they even admit those crimes exist—as 'accidents of history.' This rather unimaginative intellectual dodge simply demonstrates that these historians are scarcely Marxist. How, from a Marxist point of view, can one explain so many accidents and deviations over so many decades without finding their causes in either the economic system, the social system or the political order?" When error is acknowledged, the error is never one of doctrine, for "the 'criticisms' of socialist living conditions published in the Eastern European press, cited often by Communists in the West as proof that the East is not totalitarian, always attack the erroneous interpretation or incompetent execution of orders from the summit, never the summit itself nor its system. Error, when it is publicly recognized, is always error in execution, never error in leadership and still less in principle."[2]

At the end of one debate at the Eleventh Congress of the International Political Science Association in Moscow, I took the occasion to remind our Soviet friends that while Americans within an open society spoke with many voices on unsolved problems, we too were united in our underlying beliefs and in our determination to offer to the world the example of a good society. I may have misread their responses but I felt, for a brief moment, that my argument had struck home. American resolve in responding to Soviet aggression in Afghanistan demonstrates a commitment to values more eloquent than words, provided it is kept within bounds by a sense of realism and proportion.

Whether or not the Soviets or the Chinese perceive fully the deep-running American commitment to democratic values and goals, what the rest of the world perceives may be more important in the long view of history. It is vital that others not judge America by Watergate or Vietnam. More instructive would be assessments by friends abroad who judge Americans by the defense of freedom in the war against Hitler which followed the isolationism of the 1930s or by a two-hundred-year history of coming to the aid of the world's neediest people at times of catastrophe in their moments of greatest suffering and travail. In the immediate future, communism's promises of shortcuts to a better world may offer comfort in providing a single, all-embracing solution to every problem of hard-pressed developing countries. (In the summer of 1979 in Moscow, Soviet spokesmen hammered home the point that communism offered comprehensive answers to all mankind's problems in the writings of two political theorists, Marx and Lenin, while America and Europe had become towers of Babel with dozens of competing political theories. I could not forbear asking, remembering Trofim Denisovich Lysenko and Lysenkoism, what progress would have been achieved in Soviet science if the Russians had clung to a single scientific theory.) It is tempting for nations on the brink of economic disaster to suppose that economic determinism will save them. Yet the histories of Nazi German and Fascist Italy and the failures of Soviet agriculture throw a cloud over such sweeping oversimplifications.

Man does not live by bread alone and two thousand years of political history in the West attests to the limits of coercion. The resurgence of freedom in world history and of mankind's innate search for greater autonomy and self-rule amidst all the vicissitudes of tyrannical regimes alternately supplanted by more representative government, then replaced by new tyrannies, and finally overturned when tyranny became too vexatious, offers lessons on the relationship between the nature of man and his forms of governance. Such lessons are more profound than those of determinist economic theory. The vocabulary of contemporary political theory and the imagination of its spokesmen may be too impoverished to encompass these truths. Nevertheless, what political history teaches is that legitimacy is required for any political regime that would long endure. Consent of the governed, which is as often tacit as it is expressed in particular electoral forms, is the bedrock of legitimate regimes. When coercion, which is present to some degree in every regime, becomes intolerable, men throw off the bonds of tyranny, alone or in concert with others who cherish freedom. This longer view of history provides important correctives to the too simple short-run views that rest on superficial judgments of human nature.

Political prediction is of all aspects of politics the most uncertain; no one can read the future. Yet the political systems which have disintegrated from within and ultimately have failed have almost always rested on a one-dimensional approach to public order, whether militarism, imperialism, or, with all its strengths, Roman law. A long-lived political system must keep in proper balance justice and stability, freedom and security, and liberty and economic development. Moralism and utopianism, despite the high price they exact in human sacrifice to a single moral end and their unspeakable cruelty in pursuing their goals, present momentary fascination and attractions. In the long run, however, they fall prey to the requirements of practical morality and the balancing of competing human ends. Nothing is more hazardous than to cast aside political and moral reason in the false belief one is following the wave of the future.

Alexander Solzhenitsyn in *Lenin in Zurich* imagines Lenin's reaction to the news that the First World War had begun:

"A joyful inspiration took shape in his dynamic mind—one of the most powerful, swiftest, surest decisions of his life. The smell of printer's ink from the newspapers, the smell of blood

and medications from the station hall evaporate—and suddenly, like a soaring eagle following the movements of a tiny golden lizard, you only have eyes for the one truth that matters, your heart pounds, like an eagle you swoop down on it, seize it by its trembling tail as it is about to vanish into a crevice in the rock—and you tug and tug and rise up into the air unfurling it like a ribbon, like a banner bearing the slogan: CONVERT THE WAR INTO CIVIL WAR!
. . . and this war, this war will bring all the governments of Europe down in ruins!! . . .
Daily, hourly, wherever, you may be—protest angrily and uncompromisingly against this war! But . . . !
(The dialectic essence of the situation.) But . . . will it to continue! See that it does not stop short! That it drags on and is transformed! A war like this one must not be fumbled, must not be wasted.
Such a war is a gift of history!"[3]

Every political ideology for which right and wrong is internalized and whose standards are to be found wholly within its own ideological framework is bound to see war and human suffering as "a gift of history." Since communism proceeds exclusively by its own dialectic of history, it has no independent standard of moral judgment to measure right and wrong. Democracy may itself be driven by crusading nationalism to positions of self-righteousness and what de Tocqueville called the most garrulous imaginable patriotism. At some point, however, democracy's moral pretensions fall under the judgment of objective moral principles outside the political order such as freedom, equality, and justice. The morality of communism shaped by the dialectic of history and by the tenets of Marxist science can only be measured within an immanent moral order possessing its own inner logic. War and peace, poverty and sufficiency, order and justice are good or bad only as they serve Marxism's historic process and its scientifically determined stages of history. However much democracy looks inward, it can never ignore the higher-law principles on which it rests. Its civil rights are judged by those rights that reside in the individual outside the political order. Because the individual stands above the processes of history, the bill of rights is conceived as a means, not an end in itself. War and peace, justice and injustice must ultimately be judged in a higher court than that of a single terrestrial political ideology. Democracy goes back to a tradition of higher values which the communist ideology denies. A viable public philosophy must clarify this difference.

III New American
Dilemmas: Transcending
the Crisis of Confidence

7

Youth and Old Age:
Equal Opportunity
or Lost Horizons

The major threats to a civilization appear oftentimes within and not outside its boundaries. We have it on good authority that for America and Western civilization, the gravest dangers are internal. Abraham Lincoln wrote: "If destruction be our lot, we must ourselves be its author and finisher." Almost a century later, Arnold Toynbee identified more than twenty civilizations whose decline could be traced in part to internal factors, to the role of what he described as "internal proletariats." Toynbee attempted to show that societies broke down because their responses to challenges were faltering and uncreative. The threats that most often undermined civilizations were social class, militarism, and nationalism. The great British historian, while acknowledging that internal proletariats were influenced by economic and material objectives, argued that social, political, and religious aspirations spurred men to act. His emphasis, while not explicitly anti-Marxian—indeed he often described Marxism as a Christian heresy—was intended to broaden social thinking. He staunchly maintained that man did not live by bread alone and that responsible analysis of the human drama necessitated scholarly attention to the intangible elements of history.

Through formulations such as these, Lincoln and Toynbee help to redress the imbalance in social history. Liberals and conservatives, no less than Marxists, have been prone to focus primarily on economic factors. When I wrote an article on America's crisis and its multiple causes, a Virginia publisher editorialized:

119

We would stop at the very first word: inflation. All those other problems are real and seem "intractable" but are capable of solution. But inflation has made reasonable people tricky, calm people afraid. It has turned savers into spenders and made normally decent people act with a vicious selfishness. Get the inflation under control and the American people, as diverse as they are, can once more resemble a community.[1]

In the 1930s, the controlling assumption of much social and political thought was that improving man's economic status would solve the human problem. Given the fact that America was struggling to recover from its most severe economic depression, it was hardly surprising that economics took priority. However, the urgent problems of the 1950s and the 1960s—anomie and alienation, isolation and loneliness, McCarthyism, the youth revolution, political assassinations, urban violence, the revolt against authority, cultural malaise, reactions to consumerism, and Vietnam—all stemmed from noneconomic roots. When Erik Erikson set forth the idea of an identity crisis for younger and older Americans, he tapped a dimension of the human condition that materialist thought had overlooked. Even with abundance and affluence, suburban Americans and their children continued to suffer loneliness and despair and continued to ask "Who am I?"

The relevance of these perspectives for America's crises can be measured by reviewing some of the flash points of conflict and tension in the third quarter of the twentieth century. For the next twenty-five years, inflation and unemployment may indeed prove the most urgent problems. In the 1930s and into the 1940s, economic issues crowded out all other problems. In the 1950s and 1960s, however, the threat to America shifted more to pressing spiritual, political, and social psychological concerns and tensions. For some 10 percent of Americans, the era was one of long-delayed advances in civil rights. Significant progress had bypassed black people for a century and a half despite the nation's success in expanding social and economic opportunity. Blacks, to be sure, had claims that were as much economic as social and political, in the midst of the struggle for black identity. Their crusade cap-

tured the public's imagination at home and abroad. Beginning
with the Supreme Court decision in *Brown* v. *Board of Education*,
advances followed one another in voting rights, educational opportunities, and improved prospects of jobs and employment. Congress
passed more social legislation in the presidency of a southerner,
Lyndon B. Johnson, than in any previous administration. The
public and private sectors joined hands in a long-overdue effort to
implement the goals of the movement. By the end of the 1960s,
and particularly in the 1970s, the number of elected black public
officials at the local and national levels increased from a handful of
conspicuous black leaders to several thousand. Corporate response
to the civil rights movement led to the identification of scores of
competent men and women who moved overnight into positions
of responsibility. By the end of the sixties civil rights leaders
shifted the emphasis from establishing voting rights to the quest
for jobs and employment as the rate of unemployment for young
urban blacks remained as high as 40 percent in some large cities.
It became evident that unless substantial and continuing progress
was made unemployed blacks would constitute a potential "internal proletariat" in Toynbee's definition of that term. With all the
undeniable progress wrought by the civil rights movement, economic equality for blacks has not been achieved. Even for blacks,
however, it was at least arguable, despite the slogans of black power
and "authenticity," that social and political equality would have
to precede economic equality and constituted the greatest challenge.

Indeed it is argued that the first phase of the civil rights movement, which stressed economic and political equality, is now over.
"It accomplished and wrote into federal law . . . what every citizen
could and should expect of his country . . . [in] voting, education,
employment, housing, public accommodations, and the administration of justice."[2] The second phase lies ahead and "requires the
passage from national to individual conscience . . . to do in the
privacy of each of our lives what we profess in public as Americans." The first phase was based on protest; the second is educational and "must move family by family, neighborhood by neighborhood, city by city, state by state to accomplish on the local scene

what has been proclaimed on the national scene." However rapid and newsworthy the achievement of a new national consensus on civil rights, its consummation among men living together in a state of mutual respect will be a long and tortuous process. It cannot be purchased with massive federal allocations of funds for jobs and housing, important as that may be. True progress depends on the transformation of social attitudes and changes in the human heart. The second phase of the civil rights movement, in Father Theodore Hesburgh's frank assessment, "is not going well. The opposition has now gone underground. . . . The Supreme Court, which was the hero in the first phase, has . . . rendered . . . decisions [on segregated housing and schooling] which turn back the clock." Hesburgh concludes:

> As a result, we will be continuing, for the years ahead, bad education in the central city for the blacks, and good education in the suburbs for the whites. Has anyone thought what it means for America to have 400,000 poorly educated, in fact uneducated, blacks enter American society each year? This cannot continue unless we really want to create two Americas: one white, prosperous; one black, unemployed and frustrated.[3]

Women are the other group in America whose status constitutes a source of national embarrassment, division, and dissension. Yet if anything the movement for women's rights is more painfully complex and unsettling for the nation. On the one hand, it is indisputable that the nation has lagged in providing opportunities for what the dominant group not very felicitously has called "the weaker sex." How incongruous to defend the doctrine of innate male superiority when any schoolboy remembers the clustering of young women at the top of his graduating class.

The civil rights movement in its earliest phase benefited from an all-pervasive sense of national guilt about race. The Swedish sociologist Gunnar Myrdahl and his followers sharpened public awareness by writing in *The American Dilemma* of a nation of two societies, one rich and one poor, one white and one black. It proved possible to mobilize the rich and the powerful to help the weak perhaps because it is always easier for the strong to aid the weak out of feelings of pity and compassion. Moreover, hardheaded economic judgments on civil rights reinforced nobler instincts. Businessmen, particularly in those beleaguered cities threatened by social disruptions and urban decay, moved to the vanguard of the movement. In a word, economic self-interest and social consciousness converged in the civil rights movement.

With women's rights, any such happy coincidence of interests was absent from the start. In almost every professional and business sector, well-qualified women were viewed as rivals and competitors; the monopoly status that men had enjoyed was challenged by women's rights. The number of women in the labor force increased from 13.8 million in 1940 to 40 million at the end of the 1970s. At its center, the women's rights movement involved a struggle among equals with intense rivalry, unrestrained competition, and limited compassion. Two other factors have also clouded the issues. The job market in fields such as education has tightened as the supply of professionally trained persons has outrun demand. Economic self-interest for men conflicts with their sense of justice. Even more serious, women's rights appear to collide with the imperatives of the American family. The movement has come into conflict with deeply ingrained views that the nation's survival depends on the preservation of the family, the cornerstone of the culture. In the 1970s, less than half of the women between twenty and twenty-four were married. For the first time in the twentieth century, families were not reproducing themselves as the average number of children fell below two per family. Thus for many Americans two rights are in conflict: equal rights for women and the sacred right of the home. Therefore, women's rights, which still await legislative enactments comparable to those for civil rights in the 1960s, face a complex and uncertain future.

The adoption of the Equal Rights Amendment to the Constitution is entering its own difficult second phase. The American dilemma in the implementation of equal rights for women involves a long and painful struggle that must work itself out, neighborhood by neighborhood and city by city. In a limited sense, the struggle for women's rights is now at a stage in its history comparable to the early struggle over slavery where adversaries defended their cause on the ground of competing fundamental principles and where the moral principles of abolitionists and the economic self-interest of landowners were in conflict. Yet the resolution of this admittedly complex problem ought not to lie beyond the reach of a highly pragmatic people. A possible solution may be one that requires a case-by-case approach. Not every woman aspires to be president of General Motors nor is the goal of devoted mother and homemaker any longer the highest aim of every woman. Goals are not everywhere the same. It is as urgent that the issue of women's rights be resolved if the nation's health is to be assured as it is that the aims of the civil rights movement be realized. To set this national goal aside is an invitation to deep internal division; progress is vitally necessary in the days ahead.

THE CHALLENGE OF YOUTH

Eighteen months before his death, the distinguished educator Robert Maynard Hutchins was asked in what way he would change if he were to relive his crowded and productive life. The questioner expected Dr. Hutchins to say he would run for president or seek a place on the Supreme Court if he had his life to live over. Instead he replied he would try to make himself more available when his children sought his counsel or when they simply wanted to talk.

In one sense, it may appear incongruous to speak of the problems of youth. With the exception of minority youngsters—and even their progress in some areas has been breathtaking—American youth are better educated, more self-confident, and more influential and successful in public and private life than ever before in history. Eighteen-year-olds have the vote. The youth movement brought an unpopular war to an end and virtually toppled a government by forcing President Johnson's decision not to seek reelection. Having led a worldwide campaign of protest, a significant proportion of youth leaders accepted responsible positions in government including the Carter administration. Moreover, demographic trends have favored youth. Twenty years ago there were 30 million Americans under twenty years of age. Ten years ago the number had risen to over 80 million, and today nearly half the population is under twenty-five. Once the group in society whom parents declared should be "seen but not heard," youth today is visible, vocal, and influential in almost every public debate. As American history makes clear, no social group whether labor or management, Christian or Jews, blacks or women, or lawyers or doctors, has ever become a political force before constituting itself a critical mass in society. Nor are numbers alone sufficient; something more is needed. In the words of certain political analysts, a group must become a political culture. It must construct its own version of a civic religion. It requires folklore and symbols, legitimacy myths and rallying points and some concept of "we" and "they." Beyond all this, historical forces and events must move the group to the center of the political stage. It must seize the moment if it would move from impotence to political power.

Such a moment occurred in the 1950s and 1960s. Without the explosion of higher education in years of prosperity and affluence, along with the civil rights movement and the war in Vietnam, sheer numbers alone would not have propelled youth to a position of strength from weakness. Without the compulsion of far-reaching social change, the voice of youth might have not been heard for another decade, perhaps even another generation. It is no exaggeration to say that more earth-shaking social changes have occurred in the past quarter century than in the past one thousand years. For in a relatively brief era, all the established institutions and structures of society have fallen under questioning: the family and the church, the state and the schools. The changes that occurred in the Renaissance and the Reformation, the age of exploration or the industrial revolution pale in significance when compared with such present-day social changes.

Moreover, social change in the past quarter century has taken its toll both on a personal and worldwide plane, both in the more intimate communities of life and on a global level. The family has undergone radical changes the effects of which no one can fathom or measure. In an earlier day, most men and women joined together in the sacrament of marriage lived out their years together, whatever the tribulations. Today one out of every two marriages ends in divorce. The number of unmarried people living together

tripled in the 1970s. In yesterday's families, life began and ended
more often than not in the selfsame locality. If Americans spoke
less of the extended family system than was the custom in other
cultures, older family structures had unmistakable similarities
with one another. Then social mobility and growth of a national
economy transformed what had been a relatively closed system into
one of continuous and kaleidoscopic change and movement.

At the same time, the locus of authority became diffused within
the family. The legendary figure, the authoritarian and tyrannical
father, passed from the scene partly because professional responsibilities drew the father out of the home and partly because the
family became more and more a community of equals. Sociologists
wrote of the trend toward matriarchal families, seen dramatically
in single-parent families but also imperceptibly when the second
parent was called on to fill the void. All these trends subtly reinforced one another. As families dissolved, the moral authority of
parents was weakened. If the head of the family had failed in
keeping the family intact, he suffered the loss of prestige as a
moral example on which children could confidently base their
lives. Thus children put more and more distance between themselves and their parents at the same time the contemporary family
was in process of dissolution.

Another established institution whose authority eroded in the
1960s was the church. Following World War II, the church's position appeared measurably strengthened. Membership and attend-
ance ratios were up and growth in the early postwar years appeared
irreversible. Reflecting the ancient wartime axiom that "there are
no atheists in foxholes," returning G.I.s and their families flocked
to churches, especially the well-recognized denominations. Somewhere along the way, however, the trends were reversed. Church
leaders who had moved too far ahead of their memberships on
issues of civil rights and world responsibility found they had lost
contact with older and more conservative members. (The decline
of the National and World Council of Churches dramatized the
problem.) In the late 1960s, leading seminaries went even further
in linking educational planning with a fairly radical version of
social change. On one side, conservative critics denounced libera-

tion theology and sensitivity training, equating them with counter-culture; on the other side, social activists found the organized church the last to change in accepting the civil rights movement. Recovery was not made any easier by the rifts that sprang up within the civil rights movement itself between militants who favored violence and black power and churchmen who preached nonviolence and a continued alliance between blacks and whites. A host of other issues divided the church including those of women clergy, a more contemporary liturgy, and new social-action programs. Yet even if such rifts had not appeared, the church's position in society would have been undermined by affluence and secularism, the rise of new institutions geared totally to a theology of change, the appeals of more conservative church groups, and the passing from the scene of such theological giants as Reinhold Niebuhr and Paul Tillich. The clamour and turbulence left century-old churches perilously suspended between social activism and religious orthodoxy. It was inevitable that the church's gains in one area decimated its reputation and authority in the other. Added to this, the flight of its members from the cities turned congregations into relics of a once prosperous past. The 1950s and the 1960s became the worst of times for those churches whom history and urban migration had passed by.

The state for its part experienced what Toynbee in another context had called periods of rout and rally. In the 1930s and 1940s, it was the state that had rescued society from economic and military disaster. By the 1950s, a respected military figure waged a successful political campaign pledged to reduce the size of government. For the first half of the 1960s, President Kennedy sought to mobilize government "to get the nation moving again." Before his mission was accomplished, he was cut down by an assassin's bullet and his successor, who tried to continue the work, was a victim of the war in Vietnam. President Nixon introduced policies which his domestic advisors described as benign neglect by the state. What political ideology did not decree, Watergate made inevitable in the years that followed. With the buildup of more and more conservative thought, the public grew wary of state intervention and doubtful about state action. There was growing talk of decentralizing and devolving power. If the state had once been looked on as a savior and Good Samaritan, it came to be seen more as the enemy against which political candidates campaigned. (How ironic to find employees seeking employment by denouncing their employer.) If the state had positive connotations politically in the New Deal era, its imagery had been reversed by the 1950s and it has never fully recovered.

The fourth social institution, the school, became the battleground of the 1960s in which the war between generations was waged. Universities and post-secondary educational institutions had become the home of a substantial fraction of youth, mushrooming from under 2 million in the 1940s to 3 million in 1950 to 6.5 million by the late sixties to 8 million by 1970. Never before in American history had so large a portion of a single demographic group been gathered within one social institution. In an era of accelerated change with the breakdown of consensus having become widespread, each group looked inward for its values, each tried to become morally and politically self-sufficient. Because university youth dwarfed every past student group in size, they not surprisingly became a law and culture unto themselves. Their numbers decreed that their influence was not subordinate to any other group; their individualism in life-styles, art, and music and social mores meant they had forged their own anchors in a sea of turbulent change. It was numbers and critical mass which gave youth its influence; it was social confusion and the breakdown of the consensus on values that invited the founding of a new value system. Out of it American society was disrupted, unsettled, and transformed beyond the expectations of young or old.

At the core of every question that is raised about youth is its relation to the historic American culture. Whenever the winds of change break across the landscape, two reactions inevitably occur. Some welcome and embrace change, seeing in the replacement of the old by the new the triumph of good over evil. Others view with alarm anything that alters a familiar and accustomed status quo. By contrast a far wiser perspective on change is one that associates change and continuity. The first step in a long journey toward becoming wise about change is recognition that some major advances have rent societies asunder. Societies, as Alfred North Whitehead insisted, must combine reverence for traditions and symbols with freedom to revise them. The demands of a living culture are too great for men to be free to choose categorically between the old and the new. This is the reason simple liberalism or dogmatic conservatism are both so irrelevant in formulating national goals. If societies are to live and not decay, they must find a place for preserving traditions and then revising them when they grow archaic.

Yet the difficult task of linking change with tradition has been confounded by the conflicts and divisions within the culture. The weakening of traditional institutions has injected an element of uncertainty and doubt into their defense. Weak-hearted support of weakened institutions has marred every effort to redefine their meaning and purpose. And the prevailing intellectual and moral confusion has been reinforced by the rate of change. Tradition successfully holds societies together when its function continues to be understood. In periods of normal change, tradition can serve to channel change; for, as Paul Freund, Harvard's greatest constitutional law scholar, has written: "It is no disparagement of a work of art or of its interpreters that it takes on new relevance, yields new insights, answers to new concerns, as the generations pass. Nor is it a reproach to a Constitution intended to endure for ages to come, and to meet the various crises in human affairs or to its interpreters that it too responds to changing concerns of the society to which it ministers." *Hamlet* in successive historical periods was interpreted as a story of revenge, an inquiry into sanity, a study of mother fixation, or an example of the death wish. None of these perspectives was necessarily wrong; each possessed some validity. Indeed: "It need not be a cause of despair that to one generation the Constitution was primarily a means of cementing the Union, to another a safeguard of property, to another a shield of access to political participation and equality before the law."[4] In seeking to apply tradition, society must seek both the light it provides for guidance and the cross-lights within society. It has been possible with history and literature, law and the Constitution to be responsive to change without destroying

tradition. Merely to worship at the shrine of change is to place
too low a value on man and human nature. In William James's
apt phrase: "It is not thinking with the primitive ingenuity of
childhood that is difficult, but to think with tradition, with all its
acquired force."

For various reasons, the late 1960s proved a particularly difficult time to reconcile tradition and change. The era was one of
widespread questioning and skepticism. The traditions which came
under fire were traditions as practiced, not traditions enshrined in
venerated documents and creeds. Patriotism was condemned because it was linked with the military-industrial complex; democracy was questioned as essentially a middle class ideology; higher
education was condemned for its impersonal approach and its
sacrifice of teaching to research; families were dismissed as having
become ladders for social climbing and status seeking rather than
havens for love and renewal. The youth offensive against the
established values of society was mounted not so much against
time-honored traditions but against social practices which fell
short of such traditions.

Allowing for the merit in this endeavor and acknowledging that
the society was deserving of criticism, two other crucial questions
must be asked. First, what were the effects of the cataclysmic
changes of the 1960s on the two generations, the young and the
old, and particularly on their relationship? Second, what will be
the judgment of history on the changing role in society of the
young, on the group that some praise as the saviours of a materialist civilization and others describe as the deracinated generation?

On the first question, it is true by definition that the rate of
social change fundamentally affects relationships between the generations. Anthropologists speak of patterns of relationships falling
into various categories. In stable or so-called traditional societies
with slow rates of change, parents and elders continue to serve as
examples for their children. When change is rapid but not revolutionary, children seek their models where they can find them,
commonly from their peers. Immigrant parents who migrate to a
new country may find their old values and customs and notably
their language ill-adapted and an obstacle to their children's

advance. Far from becoming alienated and turning against their children, however, these elders commonly seek to facilitate their children's success (for example, in sacrificing for their education). When the upheavals of social change are too great, however, alienation sets in, permanent lines are drawn, and parents are unable to accept all the consequences of too rapid change or to accept it with any degree of comprehension. It is the third pattern that has transformed the rather static society of the 1950s into the troubled and anxious nation of the late 1960s. Parents have grown perplexed and dispirited by the changes in which their children are caught up. Harrison Brown, one of America's best-known scientists, has observed that the gulf between himself and his children became greater than that between himself and his immigrant parents, neither of whom spoke English when they were transplanted to a strange new culture at a relatively advanced age. What Dr. Brown was saying was that long hair and sloppy dress, vulgarity in speech and behavior, the substituting of feeling for reason, and drugs and a Bohemian way of life were further removed from his comprehension than were the old-world customs and language of his parents.

An even more difficult question to answer is what will be the judgment of history on the youth revolution which some praise and others condemn on a more or less total basis. One answer to a part of the question is that the judgments of history are seldom as all-inclusive as the first apologists or critics would make them. In straightforward language, no group is all good or bad. Or, to paraphrase Edmund Burke, there is no way of condemning a whole people. The historian's task for the decades ahead will be to sift out what is transient and enduring in the youth revolution, what will stand the test of time, and what appeared suddenly on the horizon only to disappear as suddenly. It seems reasonable to speculate that one lasting contribution of the times may be the holding of one group, the older generation, to account for the widening gap between moral declarations and social actions. With all their self-righteousness and posturing, albeit in a good cause, youth in the 1960s discovered a central truth: mankind is never as virtuous as it claims to be. In Father Hesburgh's strong words:

"The world always needs energy, imagination, concern, idealism, dedication, commitment, service. With all its problems it gets all too little of these great human qualities from the older generation."[5] It also needs reasonable criticism and constructive peaceful protest and the redress of horrible inequalities that persist in every era.

Yet to praise enthusiasm as an end in itself or to overlook shortcomings as was the custom of some apologists for the young is hardly the route to a better world. Impatience and contempt for others and oversimplified solutions to problems with a two-thousand year history are a recipe for society's disruption and decay. Youth in the 1960s tended to be "rebels without a cause," not America's best brains applying themselves constructively to the unending tasks of social improvement. The movement tended to be more active at the periphery than it was soundly rooted at its core. When critics charge youth with being a deracinated generation, they are pointing to the rootless character of both the movement's strategic and tactical approaches. It is easier to proclaim what is wrong than to draw up a roadmap to reach what is better and good.

Thus the challenge of youth is to grow wise and responsible without slackening energy, vitality, and worthy goals. That the task is formidable may be seen in the dilemmas confronting young men and women who moved from the politics of protest in the 1960s to responsibility for governance in the 1970s. Their record thus far has been mixed, their achievements mingled with faulty judgments. Yet the Republic will continue to be enriched by the degree to which they can harness noble ideas to practical policies and patient resolve. Critics need to reflect that half the nation's population is comprised of the young. It will not do to dismiss them. But the defenders of youth and especially young people themselves must learn to use both their vision and those "acquired traditions" that have made America a beacon to the world. They need before rejecting all counsel from their elders to recall the Indonesian saying: "It is a terrible thing to have a reasonable father." In all this there must be more sharing and mutual respect but also serious questioning between young and old. What went wrong in the 1960s may well have been that the challenges of youth found their elders pliant, indifferent, and unable to offer ideas for consideration in return.

OLD AGE: ESCAPING LOST HORIZONS

The life expectation of American males has increased in our time to sixty-nine years and of females to seventy-eight years. A Soviet medical scientist has published a report announcing that a life expectancy of one hundred and fifty years is attainable when medicine improves its techniques for repairing what he calls the mechanical parts of the body. Through scores of medical techniques doctors can arrest fatal malfunctioning or decay of one organ or another that not long ago were considered causes of terminal illness. The list expands exponentially: open heart surgery, organ transplant, kidney dialysis, neurological surgery, and intricate forms of surgical intervention which make use of laser beams for high precision medical actions. The proportion of older people in the population expands each year and not surprisingly men and women find themselves looking forward to increased longevity undreamed of by parents and grandparents.

With the advent of medical miracles and the prolonging of human life, the question is increasingly raised: longevity for what? On virtually every level, the population explosion poses new sets of closely interrelated questions to which answers are not yet available. Economists ask what will happen to the economy and per capita gross national product when a larger proportion of the population is nonproductive. Psychologists are troubled that older people are struggling to retain a sense of purpose. Medical men are perplexed that physical decline appears to stem less from physical disabilities than from mental health problems. Specialists on senility report that mental decline may result more from the loss of useful social roles than from organic failure as earlier diagnosed.

In simple language, old age is increasingly seen by the rich and the poor alike as essentially a mixed blessing. Perhaps the lesson America is learning is that medical and public health breakthroughs in themselves are not enough. This lesson is one that the wiser practitioners have long recognized and understood but its national shock effects on the public have still not been fully absorbed. I worked for almost twenty years alongside two dozen medical authorities at the Rockefeller Foundation. Again and again, they warned against crash programs in medicine that ignored the possibility of profound social effects. Their mindset was a result of experience, not theory, because they had lived with the consequences of past medical breakthroughs. It was improved health and sanitation that had led to the curtailment of mortality and ushered in the population explosion. Failure to look and think ahead and plan for changing demographic patterns required medical and social scientists to join in what they described as "catch-up work." Foundations and government agencies have a penchant for looking for urgent, definable problems unencumbered by disputed social theories or all the intangible dimensions of human life. Their program agendas, with a few conspicuous exceptions, are weighted heavily on the medical and public health side. It is far easier to "sell" busy trustees and beleaguered congressmen on public health targets that promise human survival than on less tangible objectives. Only belatedly, foundation officials and legislators ask themselves what are the consequences of their efforts. Medical research has about it an aura of single-minded concentration on essentials that leads men of action to push aside extraneous social issues.

To blame physicians and medical researchers for their successes, however, is to condemn a profession for doing well what society has called on it to do. An air of moral self-righteousness surrounds social criticism of researchers and doctors and subtracts more than it adds to human progress. Yet it remains true that the problems of aging are as central to society's well-being as are the problems of civil rights or of youth. Yet the lost horizons of the elderly have in the main attracted only a pitifully small measure of public attention and policy making. Older Americans are caught in an ambiguous position socially and politically. Their claims when they are voiced are attributed to self-seeking. Their allies are few and their lobbying insignificant. Their political base is severely limited and their goals lack political sex-appeal. It is tempting to dispose of the problem through actions that are largely material:

more and larger nursing homes, increased pensions or social security allowances, or lower transportation charges. Valuable as all
such public and private initiatives may be, they reach only the
visible part of the iceberg. Below the surface, the nation confronts
a profound social illness. Society is not doing well in its care and
concern for the aging. Its older people are cast aside by a society
that narrows their sectors of useful activity and callously ignores
their loneliness. A highly competitive economy and a public sector
that responds only to popular pressures and to the election returns
have made them the forgotten people. With every collective act of
social indifference to needs of the elderly, we are squandering
precious human resources. More serious, men and women still capable of living creative lives are condemned to the junk-heap of an
otherwise humane civilization. Most serious of all, national leaders
who might be expected to lead are strangely silent in mobilizing
the nation to mitigate suffering and loss.

The problem of the aging has become a national disgrace, and
we are beginning to look for the causes. Deep-running social forces
including the breakdown of the nation's traditional institutions
are major contributors to the problem. The breakdown of the
family plainly stands at the center of the problem separating aging
parents from busy children and destroying children's sense of responsibility. As the dimensions of family life narrow and are disputed, its capacity to provide comfort and sources of healing is
lessened. In a nation of strangers, the old have more and more
become strangers to the young. Modern social psychological
theories which preach doctrines of family harmony warn against
the disruptive influence of parents and grandparents intruding on
the peace and tranquillity of the home. Driven from the home,
aging parents are forced out of the only setting in which historically love and forbearance helped them surmount loneliness and
physical decline. In the same way that children are given a premature birthright (or some fragment meagerly dispensed) and
sent on their way, the elderly are pushed aside to cope for themselves or seek the help of strangers called agencies for their well-
being.

If the portraiture offered above seems overdrawn and exaggerated, the reality is not far behind. A new vision for the older population is no less vital than bold measures in the sectors that have found a place high on the national agenda in the 1950s and 1960s. If the 1950s was the decade of phase one in the civil rights movement and the 1960s the era for youth and women's rights, the 1980s may yet prove a period of growing concern for the aging. Throughout history the sporadic attention given problems of our senior citizens have coincided with years of economic distress; the pressures of inflation and economic stringency fall most heavily on fixed income groups. Years of affluence have as a rule been times of neglect. Beginning with the Townsend movement in the depression-ridden 1920s and 1930s, national energies were redirected to hard-pressed older peoples. If history repeats itself, the years ahead may find new legislative efforts and public policy initiatives to mitigate the needs of the elderly.

Yet the problem is as much spiritual as material. Before the nation can resolve the problems of old age, it must address public attention to the decline of all its major social institutions. As much as with any other social problem, the needs of the aging are interconnected with every other dimension of social life: youth, the family, the church, and the state. In the 1930s, it was not extraordinary to find the president and the Congress speaking out with concern for the aging population. How long has it been since a president spoke to the nation about the anguish and despair of older people?

Fortunately, the evidence of the sheer human capacity of senior citizens is clear to those who seek it. Volunteer service abroad, effective teaching in schools for the handicapped, and business and financial counseling are only three broad areas in which older citizens have demonstrated unique skills and talents. It will not do with the problems of the aging or with youth to dismiss their plight or ignore the challenge of the future. American civilization has much to offer its people at the beginning and end of life if it can find the will to face urgent human problems. Old lessons need to be relearned and new approaches await discovery. The stakes in these sectors are as high as with civil rights or controlling the arms race. The nation is threatened from within if it chooses the path of continued neglect. Failure here is as grim in its prospects as threats that confront us abroad. Someone, perhaps the president, must inspire national concern and find a place for these internal challenges in the context of a new public philosophy.

8

Social Problems
and Policy Strategies

The president's major tasks from the founding of the Republic have been primarily national and only thereafter international as America's influence has expanded throughout the world. The nation's first and most revered chief executive, George Washington, saw the president's first duty as bringing order at home. He warned of factionalism, disapproved of political parties, and sought to foster national unity. He cautioned against entangling alliances and opposed involvement in the wars of the French Revolution. Thomas Jefferson, who believed as fervently in universal freedom as any American president, undertook to safeguard the nation's security through augmenting its territory in the Louisiana Purchase while having recourse to the European balance of power to protect its international position. Abraham Lincoln left no doubt that preserving the union was his foremost aim although he prophesied that the cause of liberty would in the end spread to other lands. The earliest presidents saw in America's example as a nation seeking equality through liberty a guarantee of its leadership abroad. The first order of business of the Republic was putting its own house in order so that others, following our light, might discover the pathway to order and justice.

Throughout the nineteenth century, American presidents continued to speak of America's leading the world by example. Only with Woodrow Wilson did another idea gain currency, namely, that American ideals and institutions were capable of transforming the world. In Wilson's mind, American democracy and national self-determination required that democratic values be universalized and a League to Enforce Peace created that would obviate alliances, power struggles, and war. Then as the president's health and influence weakened, his dream of a brave new world was rejected by his own people. Before it could be tested abroad, the democratization of the world met defeat at the hands of the American democracy. In the decade that followed, Americans looked inward, craving normalization and a consolidation of their own strength after having been challenged, inspired, and turned back from a position of world leadership.

RETRENCHMENT AND SOCIAL PROBLEMS

For America, one approach to the resolution of its most urgent problems has been to retrench and consolidate. One administration having spent its strength in a valiant struggle to transcend the great issues of war and peace, social justice and economic disorder, successor administrations have then resolved to lower the sights. Now, weary and exhausted from the most extraordinary human effort, the American people have turned to rest on their oars. Looking inward has not always meant, however, the redirection of energies for national needs which had once been devoted to some worldwide mission. More often, normalization has entailed a slackening of resolve across the board, a pulling back from tasks which appeared too exacting on every front. When the anvil of public effort has become red hot, the president as the nation's blacksmith has rested and ceased from his labors. A people whose strengths were sapped or who imagined they could not go on have followed his example. Characteristically, retrenchment has meant setting aside the nation's most urgent problems until the nation and its leaders, renewed and rededicated, were ready to press forward once more.

THE GREAT LEAP FORWARD

An opposite approach to national problems from retrenchment is what the Chinese Communists under Mao Tse-Tung called the "Great Leap Forward," a surge of collective energy directed at what the national leadership defines as the country's most burning needs. The targets are problems which must be solved if a society is not to decline or stand still. The people are called on to give their all to alleviate some grievous wrong, some glaring social need. In the parlance of presidential government, the great leap forward is likely to occur in a leader's first one hundred days. Within a democracy, holding the public's attention on a single great issue may exceed the powers of the most persuasive leader. The strongest presidents have had the gift of calling on the people for extraordinary effort and sustaining the commitment. Weaker presidents have sought to rouse the public to a moral crusade but failed to generate the will to follow up.

Declaratory policy making has tended to falter because it has trusted too fully in the power of the word. It has also been misled into attacking a problem head-on, imagining that the best path between two points is always a straight line. Progress in ameliorating social problems is often a matter of advance and retreat. It requires trial and error more than it needs once-and-for-all solutions. Success in politics means coping and compromising, not hewing to a hard and fast line. Yet the inspirational tone of a pragmatic approach falls short of the spirit of policies defended as the moral equivalent of war. Especially in mass societies, policies which are presented as turning points or social revolutions challenge the public to act in a way that step-by-step approaches seldom if ever do. The people are likely to remain passive and apathetic until their leaders stir them to undertake major advances. Yet it has been true that if a strategy of benign neglect asks too little, the great leap forward expects too much. Neither offers a continuing basis for pursuing a steady course. Somehow a president must find a third course, but its definition and boundaries are never easy to formulate. It may be necessary to look beyond politics to find a principle that may prove helpful.

THE BALANCING OF OPPOSING IDEAS

"The test of a first rate intelligence," F. Scott Fitzgerald once wrote, "is the ability to hold two opposed ideas in the mind at the same time and still retain the ability to function." Politics and policy making constitute a realm of continuing uncertainty where no single vision will be sufficient. Politics involves not only choices

between competing goods but choices that recognize the validity
of more than one competing good. It is the president who can
deal with complexity and keep more than one social objective
steadily in view who guides policy making effectively and makes it
responsive to current problems. The "true believer" for whom
only one end or value is important is ill-equipped for political
leadership at any level.

What is true of politics is true of leadership in every other
domain. Two leaders come to mind from large organizations in
the private sector. One is a man single-minded and devoted to an
attack on a single human problem. His energy and resolve are
immense; his concentration on his one objective is complete. In
his lifetime, his efforts have ushered in a revolution of sorts. He
is celebrated for having helped bring changes that are acknowledged around the world. His assets ledger bulges with achievements; his liabilities are less numerous but not to be overlooked.
He has shown little concern for any social problem but his own
narrowly patented problem. An organization with a universal
outreach has become parochial under his tutelage. All his appointments are made in his own image. He stifles imagination in every
sphere but his own. Because of his dominance, he prefers, in his
own words, associates who are pliable. In his tenure, the quality
of staff has fallen off dramatically and the coup de grace comes in
the form of his successor, a man who proved a classic case of para-
noia. Knowing all his successor's weaknesses, the first leader embraced him because he was his own kind, not a "soft-head with
diffuse interests spread across the social order."

The second leader has surrounded himself with first-rate minds.
He has steered the organization to grapple not with one but a
dozen urgent social problems. Without lecturing his staff, whose
intelligence would turn them against a too simple moralizing, he
helps them see interconnections and the interdependence of one
social need with another. Under his direction, staff morale is high.
An impressive amount of reinforcement occurs across social sectors.
It seems unlikely that the second leader will be memorialized in
his time. One could hardly imagine him speaking of turning the
world around, perhaps because he has not staffed the organization

with image makers or high-priced staff in public relations. He writes his own speeches and is always open to new ideas. His critics charge that his efforts lack focus; his defenders see interrelationships between the several fronts on which he works. He is all too keenly aware that advance in one sector may pose problems for another sector. If his administration has not wrought a revolution in one sphere neither has it neglected urgent needs in other sectors. He will leave the organization as broad-gauged in its concerns as he found it and with stronger staff to grapple with future problems.

To translate experience from the private sector to the public domain is difficult to conceive and even more taxing to effect. Political leadership has always been leadership in a goldfish bowl; and today with the unrelenting pressures of television, it has become leadership filmed and portrayed from the privacy of the executive's most intimate chambers. The people demand not only that the president lead but appear to lead. Moreover, in a time of vast popular disillusionment, he must lead by opposing those who once constituted the elements which a president forged into an effective coalition: the politicians and bosses, the Washington establishment, senior congressional figures, liberal intellectuals, spokesmen for labor and business, bourbon southerners, and East Coast investment bankers. The president must run against Washington and govern through those he has condemned. He must pass muster not on the issues that will decide the Republic's fate but on gun control and a pro- or anti-abortion loyalty test.

A president must stand for something, we are told, but in the public arena standing for something has little to do with solving the problems. A viable policy strategy for a president who would govern calls for attention not to one but to many human needs. A president who would lead in the 1980s must prepare himself to hold down inflation while keeping unemployment below an acceptable limit. Within such limits, he must look to the needs not of a single social class but to particularly aggrieved groups. For example, he must ask what percent of unemployed is tolerable for minorities. He must struggle to find ways of maintaining economic growth rates without adding to environmental decay and the despoiling of nature's heritage. In governing, he cannot neglect either economic growth or the environment or those who are threatened most by inflation or unemployment.

Politics apart from governance requires that a political figure appeal to groups whose interests move on a single-gauged track. Industrialists are interested in growth and environmentalists in preserving the natural balance. A candidate who would be elected president cannot speak to industrialists of the environment or to environmentalists of the economic growth. If politicians learn to compartmentalize their approach, it is because, like the first type of leader from the private sector, they must appear single-minded when they reach out to single-interest groups.

In two important respects, the discrepancy between the differing strategies for politics and governance poses serious problems for a president. If he proceeds in campaigning along a series of single-gauged tracks paralleling one another but which never meet, he may gain electoral victory without ever having forged a working coalition for governing. Perhaps asking the president to mediate between the divergent elements to which he appeals and to help them identify points of convergence in their interests is asking too much. Historically, political parties and bosses have played this role, but recent electoral reforms have contributed to their decline. An incoming president having followed one strategy to victory is likely to have been incapacitated for governing.

A second problem thrown up by the political process is the threat posed by the discrepancy between politics and governance to the forming of a policy strategy capable of balancing opposing ideas. It is tempting for the "true believer," whatever his all-consuming interest, to imagine that once his social problem has been solved, society will have reached utopia. Hence sincere proponents of one goal or another are often oblivious to other social needs. However, society is so intricately joined, so interdependent from one sector to another, that no responsible leader, however intense the political pressures, can ignore society's interconnections. A policy strategy that ignores interdependencies is doomed to failure.

A workable calculus for governing demands more than anything else recognizing interrelationships between policies for urgent community needs.

Energy and inflation provide a particularly timely example of a clustering of interrelated problems likely to persist into the 1990s. Meeting the nation's energy needs in the face of rapidly escalating costs requires conservation. One of the surest means of reducing costly imports of energy from abroad is increasing costs to the consumer. The evidence from the late 1970s and 1980 tends to support this view because with higher costs, consumption fell off more than 10 percent. Policy makers in the energy field reason that further increases in price will reduce still more national gasoline consumption, although at what point the curves of necessity and economic hardship will cross is as yet undetermined.

Allowing for debate over the threshold points at which costs may or may not affect consumption, the policy strategy for energy is definable within a reasonably coherent and acceptable framework. Yet any president concerned with energy at the opening of the decade of the 1980s must be concerned still more with inflation. A single-gauged approach to energy needs clashes with the nation's yet more urgent need to bring inflation under control. Even if rising energy costs were a relatively modest portion of total inflationary pressures, a viable national policy strategy would have to relate the two. With escalating energy costs comprising by far the largest single factor in the nation's inflation, any further increase for the consumer has grave implications for inflation.

Thus the president in this vital area of society's most urgent need must fashion a politically viable strategy which balances opposing needs. Politics will push him to appeal to segments of the public exclusively in terms of each segment's most pressing needs. His task in appealing more broadly is made difficult in the absence of a widely accepted and understood public philosophy. He is more likely to announce a policy aimed at conserving energy or holding down inflation than one that tries to interrelate two of the nation's gravest social problems. Weary and frustrated Americans apparently want simplification, not talk about complexities. If it were otherwise, leading aspirants for the presidency would not year after year so grievously oversimplify. Candidates are not unintelligent. Whatever their limits, they must know better. Instinctively they recognize, however, the demands, especially on tired workers listening to ninety-second television cuts, in seeking to grasp policy strategies.

Yet if the Republic is to escape destruction from within, it must find a way to encourage its leaders to cast aside oversimplification. The evidence is indisputable that one-line proposals meant to solve urgent social problems must either result from self-deception or overweaning ambition. They must reflect a candidate's resolve to sacrifice his nation's survival to his own self-centered political success. If this is so, the people someday will rise up and overturn those who have refused to try at least to provide political strategies commensurate with the social problems to whose resolution they are addressed.

9

The Specter of Nuclear War: Two Divergent Perspectives

Early American presidents and cabinet officials lived in a wholly different world than their successors in the mid-twentieth century. The Republic's earliest presidents wrote letters and public messages by hand. Stories, perhaps apocryphal, are told of chief executives conducting the main affairs of state in half a day and spending their remaining hours reading and in conversation with close friends and family. Secretary of State Thomas Jefferson, confiding that he had made several attempts to communicate with the American ambassador in Madrid, proposed that if another year passed and he still had not heard from his envoy, he would have to take stronger action.

If the conduct of government was a leisurely and civilized pursuit in the eighteenth, nineteenth, and early twentieth century, war, as characterized by the historian Gibbon, was composed of "temperate and undecisive contests." A revolution in warfare had occurred with the passing of the wars of religion of the sixteenth and seventeenth centuries when emotions formerly directed to religion had been channeled into war and politics. The wars of the eighteenth century represented a counter-movement from an earlier era of increasingly ruthless conflict whether measured by human casualties or by the duration of conflict.

By the middle of the eighteenth century, it seemed that war, like slavery, was on the wane. Liberal intellectuals described it as an ancient social evil which was in the process of disappearing. War in the eighteenth century took on characteristics which led to its being described as a "sport of kings" fought for certain well-

146

defined and limited objectives. Wars followed a pattern of tactical and strategic moves by rival princes free of the intense nationalistic responses by the people that made their appearance in the nineteenth century. The goal of warfare was victory achieved with a minimum of engagements. Leaders constructed complicated and cunning principles for overcoming an enemy without destroying him. Court poisoners were as common as instrument of international politics and warfare as soldiers and mercenaries. The historian Guglielmo Ferrero described the eighteenth century as "one of those peaks of human evolution which man painfully attains only to slide back once more."

By the nineteenth century, war as a temperate and well-mannered pastime began to disappear under the impact of two great revolutions and social forces. The one was the French Revolution and democracy; the other was the Industrial Revolution and industrialization. The French revolutionary leader Mirabeau warned the French National Assembly that representative government was capable of becoming more bellicose than monarchy. The Industrial Revolution created new and more terrible equipment for warfare. Industrialization provided the means of warfare and democracy put a "lethal drive" into war. The humane spirit of the eighteenth century died hard in the nineteenth century. Napoleon justified the internment of British nationals by calling it "reprisal." The effects of the revolution in war were delayed. The European balance of power operated from 1815 to 1898 to control the outbreak and duration of warfare. Statistics bear out the fact that casualties were down, the relative size of armies were smaller, and the burdens of war were less. However, the late nineteenth century marked the beginning of a new trend. The moral fervor of crusading nationalism crept into the conduct of foreign policy and war and reached its full expression in the national self-righteousness of the twentieth century.

As the twentieth century unfolded, the forces that had threatened to transform war in the prior century wrought their full havoc. From the sixteenth to the nineteenth centuries, there were always periods of relative peace after an extended and costly war—in the sixteenth and seventeenth centuries after the Spanish Wars; in the

eighteenth after the wars of Louis XIV; and in the nineteenth century after the Napoleonic Wars. From the Battle of the Waterloo to
the Battle of the Marne in World War I, casualties in civil wars
were heavier than in international wars. Only in the twentieth century did Western civilization suffer a great double war in World
Wars I and II. Historians point out that the precedents for a
double knockout blow go back not to modern wars but the two
great wars of the Romans and the Carthaginians and the two struggles of the Peloponnesian Wars. What is unique about war in the
twentieth century is the fact that both materially and spiritually
war has become "total war." The distinctions between civilians
and combatants in war worked out over four centuries have been
largely obliterated. Universal military conscription has become the
rule and, with the French *levée en masse*, whole peoples have become military warriors. Moreover, total destruction is now possible,
making the evils of war virtually intolerable. War has been transformed quantitatively with the involvement of whole populations
and qualitatively with popular attitudes being directed to the total
destruction of the enemy in doctrines such as unconditional surrender. And these changes which have altered the course of four
centuries of history have taken place in a matter of decades.

WORLD WARS I AND II

World War II, for many policy makers and historians, began
with Munich, the fateful conference of 1938, when the West
capitulated to Hitler. The two leading actors of that tragic conference were British Prime Minister Neville Chamberlain and
Adolf Hitler. Chamberlain's name has become synonymous with
appeasement, and present-day leaders shrink from repeating the
fateful course that the Birmingham businessman with the umbrella
is believed to have followed. At the time, the Munich agreement
was generally applauded except in Czechoslovakia and the Soviet
Union and the four principal negotiators—Chamberlain, Daladier,
Hitler, and Mussolini—returned to heroes' welcomes in their re-
spective capitals. The main thesis of *Munich: The Price of Peace*
by Telford Taylor is that Chamberlain was no blunderer but a
moral realist; that nothing of importance was decided at Munich;

that the far-reaching decisions on Czechoslovakia's future were made first at Berchtesgaden and later at Berlin; and that the conference itself was merely "a prologue to tragedy." Taylor's thesis is that Chamberlain fervently believed that peace could be purchased, but not at any price, and that the bargain he struck failed because of the foreign and military policies of the principals, not the actions at Munich.[1]

The consequences of Munich, whatever the differences among its historians and those who applied its lessons to later conflicts, was that diplomacy became equated with appeasement and that compromise by nations became tantamount to defeat. The disparagement of diplomacy occurred at a moment in history when diplomatic accommodation had become even more vital to human survival. Two shock effects damaged the reputation of diplomacy; first, the failure of the European alliance system to prevent World War I and, second, the tragedy of Munich. Diplomacy, which has historically been linked with force as a primary determinant of peace, lost much of its credibility after World Wars I and II. Reformers heralded the end of diplomacy and its replacement by new and more rational institutions for preserving peace, including the League of Nations and the United Nations. Before World War I, the authority of established governments to seek peace and protect the nation's vital interests menaced by the threat of external force was generally accepted. The majority of the people supported governments in their determination to resist threats to national security by the use of force and to employ diplomacy in the management of international relations by negotiation. In Harold Nicolson's opinion: "The war of 1914–18 did much to change this. . . . On the one hand it was realized that a country might be committed (without its full knowledge, deliberation and approval) to policies involving definite pledges to foreign Powers. . . . On the other hand it was known that modern warfare is not confined in its effects to those professional soldiers and sailors who of their own free will have selected the profession of arms; but that it entails upon every individual citizen anxious ordeals, heavy anxieties and appalling dangers."[2]

This new involvement of the public had its positive side. It encouraged informed criticism and more continuous alertness. But in approaching the problem, the public mind grew confused. "Their alertness took the form of anxiety; their criticism manifested itself all too often in shapes of exaggerated suspicion; and their attention became strained."[3] Confusion, suspicion, and strain have persisted into the 1980s. Anxiety has swept over nations throughout the civilized world. The decline of diplomacy has coincided with the appearance of lethal weapons too terrible and destructive to contemplate. Force and modern weaponry, in the fateful phrase of former British prime minister Clement Attlee, have come to "lisp the alphabet of annihilation."

WORLD WAR III: A MILITARY VIEW

For three decades, the specter of mutual annihilation of the Soviet Union and the United States has troubled man's sleep, rising and falling in his consciousness. It is possible to chart the anxiety curve of the sleepless patient haunted by his fears without ever fully knowing the cause of those fears. Anyone striving to look beyond the fever chart is thrown into the realm of intangibles: of shifting patterns of public attitudes; of national moods; of political debates and election contests; of controversy over "missle gaps" and gains and losses in the arms race; of hopes and fears, dreams and disillusionment; of weighty personalities tipping the scales; of public response to new arms-technology priest kings; and of ambitious leaders striving to recoup their fortunes. When the fever begins to climb, the political technician can graph its ascent. His testing can probably show "who fears what and sometimes why." As with individual anxiety, the rub comes with the why. When technical men yield to diagnostic men, the layers of the problem to be studied deepen and multiply. What is needed are new forms of wisdom whenever we move from the "what" to the "why."

The "what" is not difficult to define for the 1980s. The national mood is troubled, anxious, and confused. Fear, doubt, and despair are all-pervasive. From supreme self-confidence that for every problem a solution can be found, the national vision of the future has fallen to a level of dread fear that prospective problems have outrun solutions. In this, public leaders and followers reinforce one

another. Liberals like the late Nelson Rockefeller by the close of
the 1970s had joined conservatives like Barry Goldwater in giving
expression to unrelieved pessimism. The public's concern that the
nation has declined and lost its confidence and resolve can be
charted in growth rates and inflation curves, attitude studies, and
opinion polls. Moving into the 1980s, the American people not
surprisingly have seen anxiety and fear sweep across national
boundaries. National despair, in other words, has not been contained at the water's edge. As Vietnam, Watergate, and the energy
problem have weakened America's image of its international role,
the crisis of confidence has spread to issues of national security and
the threat of a nuclear war.

The national mood helps to explain, without fully accounting
for, the British and American response to a gripping fictional
narrative by General Sir John Hackett entitled *The Third World
War: August 1985*. The cause of World War III advanced by
Hackett is more plausible than most scenarios: it came about because of Soviet opportunism and by accident. Soviet military
strength had gained the ascendancy in the late 1970s. "The warning was as clear as any given by Hitler before the Second World
War. The steady build-up of offensive military power . . . was not
only wholly consistent with a determination to impose Soviet-
Russian ends . . . by force of arms if necessary. It was hardly consistent with anything else."[4] In the late 1940s and 1950s, men
like William Bullitt and John Foster Dulles had talked about a
Soviet design for dominating the world. In the late 1970s, the
threat, as conceived by men like Hackett, was less global and universal. It was instead a strategy of unlimited Soviet opportunism
within a wide range of possible contingencies. It was "the preparation of a position of military strength from which any international
situation could be manipulated to the Soviet advantage."[5] Yet the
Soviet military buildup was threatening not only in itself but
because of the relative decline of the West in the 1970s.

The military defenses of Western countries had fallen into dis-
repair for different reasons. General Hackett is most unsparing of
his own people, noting that at the close of the Korean War in
1952 the proportion of Britain's gross national product devoted to

defense was 11.2 percent but by 1976/77 it was 4.9 percent. Britain's withdrawal from its empire had been unsettling but British national power and the nation's influence in the world had suffered most from its obsession with the redistribution rather than the creation of wealth. It forgot that national welfare depends on national wealth; it found it could no longer bear the full burden of massive trade unionism. Beginning in the late 1970s and early 1980s, slow but significant changes occurred. "A total addiction to redistributive economic and fiscal policies, which showed itself in hostility to profit-making and in penal taxation on industrial enterprise, was . . . replaced by more sensible attitudes which at last permitted an increase in national wealth."[6]

The new realism and common sense spread to other areas including national defense. Britain since its Defense White Paper of 1957 had for twenty years depended for its security on the prospect of early escalation of conflict into a strategic nuclear exchange between the Soviet Union and the United States. The concept of Britain as a conventional trip-wire setting off massive nuclear retaliation by the United States enabled the party in power to claim that it had freed the nation from peacetime military conscription. It allowed Britain to pay lip-service to such shifts in defense concepts as massive retaliation to flexible response but little else. Then currents of public concern began to flow and the reductions in defense expenditures described by military leaders as "part of the ritual liturgy of radicalism" were seen as no longer conforming to the people's wishes. A trend was reversed and by 1983 the defense ceilings of five years earlier had been exceeded by more than two-thirds.

What is prophesied as occurring in Britain in the 1980s by those who give priority to massive armament buildups is also anticipated in other countries in the North Atlantic Community. The United States will grow increasingly aware of the true dimensions of the Soviet threat. It will begin to press its European allies, strengthened by prosperity, to assure greater responsibility for their own defense. Americans and Europeans come to question whether any American president, faced with the breakdown of conventional NATO defenses, for example, in the Northern Army

Group in Germany, would risk the incineration of Chicago by employing nuclear weapons through the Supreme Allied Commander in Europe. Americans on their side will call on Europeans to review nonnuclear defense commitments—and by the late 1970s, the Europeans will respond. The buildup of Europe's defenses and American military strength at the eleventh hour assure the successful defense of Europe in World War III and lead to a brilliant victory for the West. Yet, had the United States and the European states not reversed defense policies, the Soviet Union would have triumphed.

What is clear with such scenarios is that *The Third World War* and similar books, however dramatic, stirring, and exciting, are something more than mere studies of war and national defense. Measured by intention and purpose, they are tracts and position papers on national defense policy. The moral is inescapable. Their authors are making an argument boldly and unashamedly for a renewed military effort that even in a nuclear age, even with devastating nuclear exchanges between the super-powers, can guarantee victory and survival.

Confronted with the chilling account of the causes and results and the conduct of the Third World War, students and decision makers seeking guidance are again in the presence of a profound moral dilemma. Social science and, therefore, military science as it affects foreign policy is shaped and determined by the purposes of the observer. Just as the initiative for engineering science coincided with the need for roads, the force that propels military thought is the goal of making a nation wholly secure. What makes the debate over a vast expansion in military capacity versus arms limitations so excruciatingly difficult for John Q. Citizen to penetrate is that judgments of military sufficiency rest as much on hidden assumptions as technical knowledge.

The assumptions which underlie prophecies such as Hackett's of a Third World War are five in number. Each is essential to the prophecy's validity. These military and political assumptions bear examination not because they are necessarily false but because they are interconnected; they constitute the architectural design of an all-inclusive global forecast. First, it is assumed that, given

present trends, the Soviets will attain both conventional and nuclear supremacy in the 1980s. It is self-evident that such a prospect
is one the peoples of America and Europe cannot accept. What is
called for and what can be expected is a return to the will and
resolve which led to individual sacrifice and a sustained military
buildup before, during, and after the Korean War but on the
level of higher and more sophisticated weapons technology. Even
with a major national and international military effort by the
NATO countries and America, the Soviets will be tempted to
embark on military adventures that can be turned back only by
war.

Second, and a direct outgrowth of the first assumption, the
Soviets, like Hilter before them, will use their conventional and
nuclear power to pursue foreign policy objectives in Europe. This
second assumption flies in the face of opposing estimates by experienced authorities on Soviet intentions. For example, George F.
Kennan has observed: "The Russians . . . for all their sins, and
I don't think anyone knows them better than I do, have not
threatened people with nuclear weapons. . . . I don't detect any
real intention on their part of using these weapons."[7] Another
British leader, Winston Churchill, spoke some three decades earlier,
even as he warned of Russian imperialism, that the Russians seek
not war but the fruits of war.

Third, the military prophets would have people believe that
Soviet leaders, particularly in the 1980s, will be reckless in their
military calculations, not cautious and prudent as leading political
observers have suggested. It should be noted that such predictions
are based on a succession following Brezhnev of younger and more
bellicose leaders who remember little about the heavy costs for
the Russians of World War II.

Fourth, the global political scene by the mid-1980s according to
the military prophets will find the postwar international system
in disintegration and disarray. Eastern Europe will be in a pre-
revolutionary state and India and South Africa in process of national dissolution. Jamaica not Cuba will be Russia's most dependable ally in the Western Hemisphere and Central America will
have taken a major turn toward the Communist international

orbit. The Serbs will confront the Croats and the Slovenes in Yugoslavia and will invite a Soviet invasion of their country, to which Russia will respond as the least risky military action to demonstrate its control in the Balkans and Eastern Europe. Determined to interrupt the flow of oil to Europe and America, a Soviet submarine will sink an Iranian transport and an American intelligence-gathering ship in the Gulf of Aden. Egypt, having overturned a capitalist regime in Saudi Arabia, will join that leading oil-producing country and Iraq in a new United Arab Republic reconstituted for the sixth time and linked militarily with the Soviet Union. Only Iran, which will continue to be militarily the most powerful Middle Eastern state under the leadership of the Shah, will ally itself with the Western powers.

Fifth, the new American president, a Republican southern governor elected over President Carter in 1984 will falter and, following initial Soviet military advances outside its own territorial boundaries, will accept a standstill and a false detente carrying more than a hint of Chamberlain's Munich. The Soviets having tested the new American president and found him wanting, as they had his predecessors before him, will launch a military invasion in support of the Soviet-inspired Committee for the Defense of Yugoslavia and follow it in the summer of 1985 with military action in the central region of Europe. By then, the die will be cast and World War III will be a reality.

The newly elected fortieth president of the United States whose inauguration will take place in January, 1985, will be ill-prepared for the crisis and will "need help." The weekend after the election, the president-elect will accordingly call to his home in South Carolina two prestigious advisors, not from the Trilateral Commission or the Council on Foreign Relations in New York—he had campaigned against the "soft-centered international liberalism" of the Democrats—but the director of the United Universities Think Tank and a former secretary of state. The two will warn of violence by urban guerrillas in the Third World, of potential coups d'état, and of likely dictatorial succession in all but 35 of the 180 governments of the world. The Think Tank director will outline for the president the alarm signals of instability and change in the "poor south" that the Soviet Union can be expected to exploit. He will identify four categories of nations in the "poor south": a few breakthrough countries with rising gross national products such as Brazil, Singapore, and Malaysia; a certain number of unstable right-wing countries including Mexico and Argentina in South America, the richer states of the former Union of South Africa, and the capitalist half of the disintegrating Indian Union threatened by labor strife and urban violence; a group of "unstable left-wing" countries now including most African countries, Egypt, Pakistan, Bangladesh, and the poorer states of a disintegrating India; and a number of Moscow-oriented communist countries clustered together in the Caribbean and led by Jamaica and Cuba with a few "unstable left" countries like Egypt moving toward the USSR. However, a few small countries in East Asia (Vietnam, North Korea) still calling themselves communist will have been drawn into the Japanese-Chinese East Asian co-prosperity sphere. Meanwhile, the Asian republics of the Soviet Union will be growing increasingly restless and will show signs of forging economic ties with the China-Japan co-prosperity sphere, loosening Moscow's hold on them.

The Think Tank report will identify the flash points of international conflict: Egypt in the Middle East fomenting coups d'état in Saudi Arabia and the Gulf with Soviet help; communist governments in the Caribbean and unstable regimes in Central America trying to overthrow a dynamic new president in Mexico; Zimbabwe and Namibia supported by Cuban, Jamaican, and perhaps Soviet volunteers leading military and political incursions and attacking the remaining right-wing governments of the former Union of South Africa. By contrast, the former secretary of state in his report will find the flash points of conflict in crises breaking out to the west, east, and south of the Soviet Union generated by the growth of nationalism in Russia's Asian republics and the pull of the Japan-China economic miracle; unrest created in Poland and Yugoslavia by dissatisfactions and divergences from Soviet norms; awareness in East Germany that even with its vaunted economic superiority in Eastern Europe and a GNP per head of $4,000, twice that in European Russia, it lags behind West Germany's

$11,000; and lack of security in the remaining three-quarters of the world because of Soviet nuclear superiority and the ineffectuality of SALT.

The world in the worst-case scenario is a global battlefield and although the military analyst may speak of laying part of the blame for continuing instability on the persistent Soviet-U.S. military rivalry, he looks for salvation in clearcut American victories and successes. A third world war, he predicts, will break out only if two or more of the main points of instability around the world reach a crisis stage at the same time. Only then will the international system become overloaded, as with simultaneous crises in Yugoslavia, Europe, or the Middle East. Events would then move out of control. Confronted by multiple crises, the Soviet empire would begin to crack under its own pressures and its dissolution would be set in train.

In all this, the military analyst looking into the future sees the resolution of the Cold War in terms of outright victory and defeat. His objectives are tangible, his expectations unambiguous. He arranges the world in neatly ordered categories: right, left, and center, stable and unstable, dictatorial and democratic. Columns form of friends and enemies and of "unstable" regimes crossing over from one to the other. The military mind is best equipped to advise the people whether we are ahead or behind in the arms race. Its judgments carry conviction for those who are impatient with "soft-centered internationalists." Yet the Cold War and the arms race occur in a setting in which intangibles, not tangibles, dominate, and this is the sphere in which the prophecies of most military experts are consistently wide of the mark. Looking at the Middle East in the mid-1970s until as late as 1978, the military observer understandably saw in the Shah's Iran the linchpin of a noncommunist world order. For every index based on tangible factors of international politics—tanks and guns, missiles and aircraft, and voluminuous blueprints for modernization and social reform—Iran, as President Carter declared, was the bulwark of progress and freedom. Yet the dominating forces in the area proved to be the intangible forces that swept across society. It was not the Shah's planes and guns nor long overdue reformist plans but deep hatred and resentment, envy and dislike, Islam and Khomeni, expressed in the emotions of rural peoples and the young, that swept all the tangibles before them. So unprepared for these social and cultural changes was the experienced military observer that in chronicling the end of the war of 1985 in the Middle East he could write: "The success of Iran in the Persian Gulf and southern Arabia had been such that even before the nuclear exchange in Europe precipitated the end she was already concentrating forces on her northern borders for the invasion of the Soviet Union."[8] If military prophecy in forecasting the future has failed more conspicuously it is difficult to recall the example.

Beyond its preoccupation with hardware and tangibles, the military perspective may often be misled by employing the worst-case scenario. In order to justify optimum military preparation, it appears to ask itself "what are the worst possible circumstances militarily our side could face?" Having made this assessment, the military spokesman not surprisingly demands the military means and the weaponry for survival in the worst-case situation. Given their addiction to the worst-case psychology, militarists view concessions or compromises as an invitation to destruction and defeat. It is precisely this psychology that conditions those who oppose arms agreements, whether SALT I or SALT II or any future agreement. It would be the height of unrealism to imagine militarists ever changing their approach when their vision of the world's political scene remains intact.

One other factor sharpens the dilemma: the indisputable fact that knowledge is preferable to ignorance in the nuclear age. The uninitiated soon flounder in weighing the alternatives of throw weight and warheads; military authority must be brought into play. The tragic dilemma reflected in books by military leaders, from Admiral William D. Leahy's *I Was There* or the writings of General Curtis E. Lemay to *The Third World War*, is that without hard military expertise and data which is uniquely the province of military men, comprehension of the harsh struggles in world politics soon exceeds public understanding. Thus the president needs military help. Yet at the same time, specialized knowledge, whether military or any other, illuminates only part of reality. The military factor can never be isolated from a wider social and political context. Thus the wisdom of any military leader, while necessary for understanding the threat of World War III, is inescapably insufficient. The general, having moved beyond the boundaries of his military competence, is as helpless in grasping social and political trends as the nonmilitary mind is in comprehending military necessity. At some point there must be a union of the two but it is a union that becomes ever more difficult. The failure of most portraits of the Cold War results not from lack of clarity and precision with which the military interpreter sketches in the details of the conflict. It results from the limits of his political and diplomatic knowledge and the impossibility of political prophecy.

NUCLEAR WAR AS AN ABSURDITY

Arrayed against the viewpoint of the military observers identified above is that of the political scientist who argues that nuclear war is an absurdity. To contemplate it as a practical alternative in foreign policy is to deceive ourselves. In the past, war was properly seen as a continuation of policy by other means. It was a rational enterprise. Today's nuclear weapons are instruments of total destruction. Not only do the traditional laws of war no longer apply but in a nuclear war there will be only defeated nations. One nuclear warhead, it is said, is technologically capable of contaminating for generations to come all of the Middle East's oil fields or that part of the world's food supply produced in the American Middlewest. Nuclear war, given its total destructiveness, is not a rational enterprise.

The nuclear phenomenon, for those who see it as nonrational, has created a gap between the way policy makers think and act and the actual conditions under which human survival must be pursued. The only way to deal with nuclear weapons is to deter and prevent their use. The lethal instruments which threaten mankind's destruction pose qualitatively different issues for states. Therefore, it is fallacious in approaching arms negotiations to speak in the vocabulary of conventional disarmament. Wars in the past have always been based on a "military economy of scarcity" (Hans J. Morgenthau) in which the number of possible targets far exceeded the number of weapons. Every serious attempt in the nineteenth and twentieth centuries to bring the arms race under control under such conditions has failed. By contrast today's efforts to put a lid on the arms race are being carried on under a "military economy of abundance." With the number of weapons far greater than the number of targets, there is an immense over-kill capacity. It is beyond man's imagination to comprehend fully the implications and consequences of so revolutionary a change, in part because the problem remains largely an abstraction. Men have had no experience with the use of the latest, most powerful thermonuclear devices.

Despite the terrifying prospect of mutual annihilation, certain leaders on both sides of the Iron Curtain have increasingly talked of surviving and winning a nuclear war and the thinking reported above illustrates this trend of thought. Scientists like Edward Teller and military leaders like Air Force General George J. Keegan, Jr., have pointed to civil defense programs in Russia and China as evidence that viable defense systems were possible. The political scientists who oppose this kind of thinking maintain that talking glibly about evacuation and civil defense is an illusion. Russian civil defense provides only for protecting the highest levels of the political regime with no significant protection for the great mass of the people. These critics minimize, as do scientists like George Kistiakowsky of Harvard, the viability of civilian defense and go on to argue that even those who survived a nuclear strike would emerge into a contaminated environment threatening continued human existence.

Therefore, any American president faces an awful and perhaps insoluble dilemma. War between the superpowers would under existing conditions be suicidal and genocidal. Responsible leaders in power recognize this constraint and are nearly helpless in using force to achieve their ends. Only politicians out of power can ignore the dread threat of mutual extinction and call for reckless acts by their nation. In the past, America would not have hesitated to bring the full weight of its military arsenal to bear in a crisis such as Iran. Because of the nature of the crisis and the importance of Iran and the Middle East in the Cold War, it has been necessary to exercise immense restraint, to call in every international agency such as the United Nations and the International Court of Justice, and even seek to bribe its "enemy" with promises of foreign aid and a full-scale investigation of past misdeeds. Successive presidents, beginning with Eisenhower and ending with Ford, faced comparable restraints so far as employing all available American weapons in Vietnam. When American secretaries of state have reached the end of their public service, often the one achievement for which they have claimed credit has been the prevention of nuclear war.

Whatever the actions of responsible leaders, the public, with encouragement from some aspiring political and military figures, continues to think in conventional terms about war with the Soviet Union. They view it as a practical alternative, whereas they ought to recognize that a war between the superpowers would likely incinerate the world. No one would be the victor; everyone would lose. Somehow a president must persuade or force the public to think more realistically about the largely incomprehensible dangers of nuclear warfare. He must help shift public thinking about solutions from its conventional to unconventional patterns. Mankind's survival may depend on facing up to a tòtally new and unprecedented situation.

In the debate between those who urge larger and larger arms buildups and those who press for arms limitation, the president must warn that given history's lessons, nuclear weapons like all previous weapons are being developed not to be stored but to be used. Those who defend their manufacture and production are likely to call for their use in one or the other future crisis. The likelihood will be the greater in proportion as leaders see them as essentially no different than any other weapon. It will not be enough for future presidents to show restraint; they must help the public to understand why restraint is a necessity. For the public must find ways of holding popular passions in check and preventing conflicts from approaching the catastrophic conclusion of nuclear war. The Soviet Union and the United States as the princi-

pal rivals in the Cold War have many interests which are in conflict. Fortunately they have one interest in common and that is
their interest in survival.

The viewpoint of political and diplomatic observers like Hans
J. Morgenthau and George F. Kennan that nuclear war is an
absurdity clashes with that of military observers like General
Hackett. The two outlooks are antithetical and cannot easily be
resolved. An incumbent president cannot escape choosing between
the two perspectives as they influence policies on arms control and
the military defense budget, however he may apply them in practice. It is a truism that broad viewpoints provide ways of looking
at concrete problems. They don't offer blueprints that give ready-
made answers to specific policy choices. Yet to ignore the implications or probable consequences of one or the other viewpoint is
to be mislead. Those surrounding a president and the chief executive himself are likely to be dominated in their thinking by one or
the other trend of thought. It will not do to argue that ideas and
theories hardly matter if it remains true, as the political scientist
Max Lerner wrote, that "ideas have consequences." In no other
sphere are the consequences greater than on issues of nuclear
strategy and policy. Yet if the stakes are great, the unknowns are
even greater, and to bet on one or the other nuclear viewpoint is
to venture a choice with the most momentous significance for
human survival.

PROPHECY AND HUMAN SURVIVAL

Failures in political prophecy are, of course, nothing new. History
records countless examples of decisive political developments that
caught even the most experienced observers by complete surprise.
In the eighteenth century neither Benjamin Franklin nor Frederick
the Great appears to have anticipated the approaching French
Revolution, yet both were constant observers of the course of
French affairs. Nor did someone as active in revolutionary politics
as Madame Roland make a single allusion before 1789, in her
voluminous correspondence to the impending downfall of the
French monarchy. Napoleon was confident that "Europe will be

either Cossack or Republican," and Pitt prophesied that the end of the papacy was in sight.

Political prophecies concerning foreign states have most often fallen short of the mark. The knowledge that people possess of the social and political conditions of another country is almost always so imperfect and superficial, so circumscribed and confined by parochialism, that popular generalizations tend to go widely astray. In 1760, Rousseau predicted that in twenty years England would be ruined and have lost her liberty. The statesmen of Europe joined philosophers such as Rousseau in proclaiming England a decadent and second-class power, a sort of insular Poland, selfish, faction-torn, without nerve and consistency, and destined to fall under Russia's domination. The illusion that England was fast declining was shared by Joseph II of Austria, Frederick II of Prussia, and Catherine II of Russia. These erroneous estimates provided the groundwork for far-reaching policies which affected the future of the world. Most fateful of all, the Kaiser and Hitler underestimated both Britain and America and chose courses that changed the history of the West and of the rest of the world as well.

If these experiences carry any lesson for the present, it is that future events may be decisively shaped by the political estimates of America or Britain or Russia or India or Japan or China or Poland or Yugoslavia being formulated as a basis for contemporary foreign policies. It is also true that estimates regarding military strategy such as France's dependence on the Maginot Line can deliver up a people to military defeat. Even more than military estimates, however, political and diplomatic prophecy is the scene of tragedy and failure for prophets, whether soldiers or diplomats.

The president needs help as he looks ahead to the grim prospect of World War III but the question for any president must be "whence cometh my help?" He cannot ignore the implications of contending viewpoints on the nuclear problem yet he can never be wholly confident he is following the most prudent course. He must measure the intentions and capacities of friend and foe without being certain he has plumbed the depths of the mainsprings of action in a foreign country about which he is doomed to remain a stranger. And to all the historic complexities of political prophecies and the uncertainties of the balance of power he must add the mysteries of the balance of terror. The people can only ask of its leaders the political and moral courage to make choices not on the basis of partisan advantage but with a clear-eyed understanding of the enormous change which nuclear technology has introduced in the making of foreign policy.

IV The Future and the Presidency

10

The Decline and Fall
of America:
Prophecy Reviewed

The climate of political discussions in America, which in the 1940s and 1950s had reflected hope and anticipation, darkened and clouded over with doubt and uncertainty in the 1970s. National morale was shaken and undermined by events that troubled the American psyche and weakened what critics had warned was the false optimism of the decades immediately following the Second World War. This dramatic shift in national mood reflected more than changing trends in political thought for which intellectuals must bear responsibility. In the 1970s it became fashionable to charge that intellectuals had suffered a loss of faith and will. Neo-conservative journals such as *Commentary* and *The Public Interest*, to say nothing of *the National Review*, and writers such as Irving Kristol, Norman Podhoretz, and Senator Daniel Patrick Moynihan, stridently charged that liberal intellectuals had grown faint of heart. Such publicists see the growing despair and disillusionment with America's future as essentially an intellectual problem. They argue that the writers who spoke out in defense of American democracy and its values in the aftermath of the Second World War lost confidence and resolve in the aftermath of Vietnam and Watergate. They prophesy that unless American intellectuals recover their devotion to freedom, the nation will decline and fall.

This view of the direct and dominant role of contemporary intellectuals in shaping public attitudes in the immediate present as contrasted with their long-run influence on civilization is not entirely persuasive when considered against broader perspectives in the history of thought. Intellectuals may indeed be the legislators of mankind, but it is difficult to call up the name of any political thinker who in the short run has had so pervasive an effect on mass attitudes and popular moods. By contrast, it is possible to enumerate a handful of leaders—Lincoln in the Civil War, Roosevelt in the 1930s, and Churchill in World War II—whose words shaped or channeled public emotions and stemmed one kind of popular response or generated another. Intellectuals for their part have performed different functions. Some have merely reflected and mirrored the spirit of their times. In so doing, they have helped the people articulate their feelings, commitments, and aspirations. Others have been social critics and stimulated the re-thinking of prevailing modes of action and thought. In large measure, however, the dominant influence of intellectuals has been through ideas that have lived on after they were gone. The implications and effects of their ideas have awaited interpretation, translation, and restatement by others to accord with new realities. As we have seen (see p. 78), Abraham Lincoln helped Americans understand more fully the political principles Thomas Jefferson enunciated. Moreover, a direct line between thought and action was more commonplace in an earlier and simpler age. The principles laid down by the founding fathers were written into the Declaration of Independence and the Constitution. To discover analogies through a comparison of present-day political thought and practice with the influence of early political writings is questionable. We remain too close to our own history; the crisis of our time cannot be attributed exclusively to the impoverishment of political thought.

The mood of a nation of 230 million people, whose interests and attitudes are fractionated by vast regional, ethnic, social, and economic differences and whose thinking is shaped in many complex and intangible ways by the media, is a difficult phenomenon to assess. Today's social climate is the product of many forces. Its ebb and flow follows cycles that are as often irrational and unpredictable as they are the product of rational determination. The public mood reflects surges of popular emotion which oftentimes seem to have only a tangential relationship with political and social realities. For example, the public's anxiety over the workings of the economy bears little relationship to its overall vitality or sick-ness. In 1973 and 1974, the effects of the boycott of Middle East oil produced what almost every observer described as a breakdown in confidence in the American economic system. America suffered what was perhaps its most crippling and embittering postwar re-cession. At the same time that the public was seized with fears and doubts, however, investors from oil-rich countries were channeling their newly acquired surplus capital into the American economy. Apparently, the public's loss of confidence stopped at the water's edge. Or to cite another example, the administration of John F. Kennedy came to power on the heels of a fiercely conducted elec-tion campaign in which Democrats charged Republicans with re-sponsibility for a missile gap between the Soviet Union and the United States. Apparently Soviet leaders viewed the strategic balance in a different light because the nuclear superiority of the United States in the early 1960s is credited by historians as being responsible for the Soviets' removing their missiles in 1962 from Cuba. The abortive invasion of Cuba at the Bay of Pigs was followed by resolutely effective responses of the Kennedy admini-stration in ending the Cuban missile crisis. In the mid-1970s, a president who had normalized relations with China, the most populous nation on the face of the earth, resigned in disgrace following Watergate. And in the late 1970s, the deteriorating strategic position of the United States which has aroused wide-spread public fears has not prevented the Soviet Union from making important concessions in SALT II that would have seemed unlikely if the United States was as weak as critics have pro-claimed. (Would the Soviet Union have negotiated for seven years with a paper tiger?) The tide turned in 1979/80 when SALT II was shelved following a massive attack by former military officials and their friends in the Senate arguing that America was in a position of strategic inferiority. This dissension was coupled with Soviet regional aggression in Afghanistan. Public moods and emo-tions appear to have a life of their own that unquestionably bears some relationship to external forces but is only partly determined or explained by them.

The rise and fall of nations demands closer scrutiny than little bands of intellectuals by themselves can provide. Each observer catches a glimpse or has a small vision of the far larger picture. As Theodore H. White explained: "What a reporter like me could see was only what a man in a small boat can see of the ocean— ripples or whitecaps or great breakers, the surface as the wind moves it, not the powerful tides nor, underneath them, the irre- sistible sea currents." History is composed, as is the ocean, of waves, tides and currents; the calm on the surface may conceal deep-running waters or its visible turbulence may result not from the waters but from passing winds. "A sequence of events is like a series of waves, one crest following upon another; and the trick, for statesman and reporter alike, is to tell which crest is a surge of the tide and which a mere accident of the wind."[1] In judging the past or looking ahead to the future, no task for a statesman is more exacting than judging the tides.

Beyond the complexities of charting the waters of history and distinguishing between their transient and persisting directions, the place of the historian and the interpreter sets limits to the individ- ual's understanding. The intellectual who seeks to make sense of the apparently senseless movements of history does so within the limited boundaries of thought of one individual or one ideology. He is constrained by his own knowledge and hemmed in by his assumptions. Liberalism leads down one path and conservatism another. One strain of liberalism pushes him to defend tolerance and reason and to attribute breakdowns in the culture to lack of free discussion. Another form of liberalism explains economic and social decay by failures to maintain the free market system. Con- servatism and neoconservatism in particular calls for restoration of civility, less emphasis on egalitarianism and more on meritocracy and resistance to the breeding out of intellectual and political aggression in privileged classes. The problems that confront the different ideologies in the present crisis are not in dispute: the breakdown of trust, the weakening of institutions, the dissolution of values, casual amorality, the retreat from civic consciousness, and the widespread disappearance of a sense of responsibility. Yet when- ever interpreters move from description to diagnosis and prescrip- tion, the dominating effects of their intellectual positions shape their conclusions. It may be comforting to be told that a new class of intellectuals or "policy professionals" can resolve this dilemma, but there is scant evidence that this will be the case.

THE FORTIES

History follows a pattern of cycles that can be broadly associated with the decades in American history. With certain exceptions, a decade of dramatic activity has been followed by one of regrouping, rebuilding, and consolidation.

The 1940s, like the 1930s, were America's "time of troubles" and a decade of global testing. As the trials of the 1930s were economic, the crisis of the 1940s was international. Hitler had prophesied that America would not enter the war. He had said the Americans cannot swim, the Americans will not fight, the Americans will never come. The controversies which preceded America's entry into World War II were deep and bitter. One group of Americans charged President Roosevelt with having drawn the nation into war and with having deceived and misled the people. Another group praised him for his vision and leadership. It would be more accurate to say that the administration, including the president's closest advisors, were ahead of the public in sensing the threat to the national interest in Hitler's march through Europe. Yet they tried not to move so strongly as to lose public support. As was characteristic of Roosevelt's leadership, he sought, consummate politician that he was, to nudge public opinion toward support for the war. Without entering the debate over his tactics, the student of international politics can safely assert that America met the test of world leadership in the Second World War. Not only did the nation help to forge the Grand Alliance, but the consequences of the struggle were victory and the emergence of the United States as the mightiest superpower in the postwar world.

For those who were not part of the wartime and early postwar experience, it is difficult to recapture the emotions of the time. With all the fears and uncertainty about the survival of freedom and the outcome of the war, the 1940s were years of dramatic challenge and response. Seldom in American history had the nation responded so resolutely and decisively. If the triumphs of World

War II are viewed as America's finest hour, the mobilization of the nation in peace after 1947 was not far behind. Following rapid demobilization, the United States was confronted by a new threat: Soviet Russia took the place of Hitler's Germany. Historians wrote of the "brave and essential response of free men to Communist aggression."[2] President Harry S. Truman, who came to office ill-prepared for the momentous tasks of world leadership, rose to the challenge, and displayed qualities of decisiveness and courage for which he will always be remembered. In a momentous fifteen-week period, the Truman administration hammered out policies that constituted a turning point in history: the Marshall Plan and the Truman Doctrine, and later the North Atlantic Treaty Organization. A nation whose peacetime policies had for the most part been isolationist engaged its strength around the world. The span of time required for this revolution in American foreign policy was unbelievably brief. Herbert Feis has written: "By the end of 1945, the war was won and hopes were high. By the end of 1949 these hopes had crumbled. . . . Mutual trust had gone, mutual terror was becoming the decisive restraint."[3]

Trust in a principal wartime ally was replaced by terror because leaders, who had believed that the end of war heralded the dawn of a new age of peace and harmony, concluded that Stalin and the Russians understood only the language of power. The task of the nation's leaders shifted from proclaiming utopia to rousing the citizenry from a mistaken illusion that the defeat of Germany, Italy, and Japan had ended world conflict. The spokesmen for a new American foreign policy addressed the Congress and the citizenry not in the measured tones of statesmen or diplomats but as protagonists on the campaign trail. They undertook and succeeded in awakening the public from its lethargy and inspiring a national consensus that was channeled into far-reaching new policies. The "we" and the "they" in foreign policy were clearly identified as the United States and the Soviet Union; the world struggle was cast in a mold of democracy versus international communism. Promissory notes were offered as justifications of the new foreign policies that containment of the Soviet Union through NATO and the Truman Doctrine would lead to the elimination of communism in Europe. Privately, the defenders of NATO and the Truman Doctrine acknowledged that they were claiming too much for their policies but maintained that their overstatements were necessary to build support in Congress and the nation.

Thus the nation discovered a common unifying purpose in the mid-1940s. It more nearly approximated the national purpose in wartime than in any period following World War II. The public coalesced behind its leaders in a struggle that was widely interpreted as likely to determine the fate of mankind. Full-scale war pits nation in arms against one another; it unites a whole people around common symbols and goals. For a nation at war, society is purged of conflicts and differences; national unity reaches its pinnacle. The Cold War differs from open warfare and involves elements on contradiction and conflicting values. It has been marked by debates over ends and disputes over means and policies. The last half of the 1940s were an exception; national unity emerged in the decision to resist worldwide communism. Politics and foreign policy found a center in the belief that monolithic worldwide communism constituted the enemy; national energies were mobilized to turn back the foe in conflicts which were less than hot war but which involved a protracted struggle.

The consequences of such a crusade against world communism were far-reaching for the society, the nation, and the economy. The economy, which had expanded during the war (the United States was the only major belligerent whose GNP increased in World War II), continued to grow. As war had been a stimulus to the economy, the Cold War took up the slack that some economists had predicted was leading to a postwar depression. The economic incentives resulting from the rebuilding of Europe and from providing assistance to countries like Greece and Turkey that lay in the path of Russian imperialism led to continued economic expansion. It is unnecessary to join the revisionist school of Cold War historians who explained every postwar American policy as resulting from capitalism's frantic scrambling to gain markets in Western and Eastern Europe to recognize the economic importance of the Cold War.

Similarly, the explanation of the Cold War as a struggle between democracy and communism gave such diverse groups as labor and management, Catholics and Jews, reactionaries and socialists, the military and the industrialists, and liberals and conservatives a common rallying point to which lesser differences were subordinated. From the first days of the Bolshevik Revolution in 1917, nearly every major social group in America had been anticommunist, although they expressed varying degrees of antagonism to the communist foe. Once the Soviet Union and worldwide communist expansion were identified as the enemy, these separate groups united in support of what critics like Walter Lippmann described as an anticommunist crusade.

The lessons of the 1940s are unmistakable for those who seek to explain the search by Americans for a common national purpose. The first lesson points up the importance of a common enemy. A people are more likely to band together in the face of a threat from the outside by a nation or a group that is defined as "they" in opposition to a "we." The colonists united in the eighteenth century in the struggle for independence against Britain. The Soviet Union created a communist political system that has maintained itself in power by claiming to be threatened by capitalist states. The newly independent nations in Africa and Asia have achieved political unity by preserving the myth that they continued to be threatened by the colonial powers. Writers on world order have maintained that the only sure path to international unity would be the appearance of an enemy from beyond the planet who challenged global survival. In the thermonuclear age, some students of world politics have argued that nuclear weapons might bring nations together in a single world government. From the 1940s, Americans can learn that negative forces embodied in an external threat were important in molding national or international unity and creating a common purpose.

Another lesson to be drawn from the experience of the 1940s is that a common national purpose may partake of what the historian Jacob Burckhardt called the "grand simplification" of history. The legitimacy myths on which nation building has proceeded have tended to be oversimplifications on which a whole people could rest their understanding of political and social reality. What

Professor Joseph Schumpeter wrote of the Marxian theory of imperialism is also descriptive of other operative political theories: "A series of vital facts of our time seems to be perfectly accounted for. The whole maze of international politics seems to be cleared up by a single stroke of analysis."[4] Imperialism, which serious studies demonstrate is not determined alone by economics, international bankers, or other personal devils, is for Marxists, who have a single all-inclusive theory, explained by a "grand simplification." Indeed: "The rule of the financier . . . over international politics" is in the words of Professor Schumpeter "a newspaper fairytale, almost ludicrously at variance with facts."[5]

In the spirit of Schumpeter's critical comments, the definition of the enemy in the 1940s viewed historically was a gross oversimplification of political reality. The real threat to the vital interest of the United States was Russian imperialism, which, given the policies of the Soviet Union, would have constituted a threat whether or not it was driven forward by the dynamics of Tsarist Russia or by communist political ideology. The postwar map of the world was pockmarked by what the best-informed observers called "political empty spaces," especially in the heart of Europe. The threat to the balance of power was inherent in the power of the Soviet Union spreading into political vacuums. It was vital that Russian imperialism be resisted, and with the decline in the power of Britain and the nations of Europe, responsibility fell to America to hold back Soviet expansion. Unquestionably the threat was greater because Stalin harnessed communism to Russian imperialism, not abstract world communism. History was to shatter the illusion of a monolithic communist system controlled and directed from Moscow. In the 1940s, however, congressional approval of a massive economic and military commitment by the United States to the defense of freedom against communism apparently required a simple formulation of democracy engaged in a worldwide struggle with communism. Americans found a common purpose in the vision of freedom-loving people defending themselves against what policy makers depicted as the international communist conspiracy.

The third dimension of national unity in the 1940s was the

widespread belief that economic growth and personal affluence would assure human happiness. Despair in the 1930s appeared to stem from economic dislocation and deprivation. The economic system was not working and respected observers prophesied the demise of capitalism. It was natural, therefore, that the underlying assumption of social reform in the depression and postdepression period was that improving the individual's material circumstances and the society's economic health was a precondition of every other advance in American society. Almost no one disputed that strengthening the economy came first; few appeared to doubt that improved standards of living would lead to improvements in the quality of life. The 1940s, and especially the second half of the decade, were years of affluence and abundance. The nation was not only actively anticommunist in its external relations but buoyantly self-confident that its material advances would benefit all its citizens. There was a commitment to numbers: more jobs, more students in universities, and more church members. For most Americans, more was equated with better. Thus internally as well as in foreign relations, the nation appeared held together by the cement of a common purpose which was widely accepted but which came under scrutiny in the decade that followed.

THE FIFTIES

The 1950s began as a continuation of the 1940s. Two events occurring early in the decade have been widely interpreted as high watermarks in the Cold War: the Korean War in 1950 and the defeat of the French in Indochina followed by the Geneva Conference in 1954. With regard to the former, the invasion of South Korea by troops from North Korea was seen as confirming the theory that monolithic world communism constituted a global threat to international peace and stability. The evidence was unmistakable that North Korea had launched its attack on the South with the approval and support of the Soviet Union. The fact that American leaders such as Secretary of State Dean Acheson and General Douglas MacArthur in formal policy statements and informal interviews had seemed to place South Korea outside the defense perimeter of American strategic military commitments may have tempted communist expansion. In any event, the fact of communist aggression blatantly pursued in Northeast Asia offered proof to those who doubted that the communist blueprint for conquest was global in character. It lent support to the view that worldwide actions were initiated at a single switchboard. The defeat of the French in Indochina and the agonizing choice for America called on to take up resistance to communism in Southeast Asia led to the Geneva Conference in 1954. There Soviet, Chinese, European, and American negotiators searched for solutions to an independent Indochina but with the American secretary of state, John Foster Dulles, choosing not to sit at the table with high communist officials and leaving the negotiating to the senior American diplomat, U. Alexis Johnson, who had little authority other than the power to say no.

Through the 1940s, the United States had maintained its traditional European focus. In Asia, its interests had been confined to the reconstruction of Japan and the support of Chiang Kai-shek's Nationalist Chinese government. American anticolonialism first caused tensions with France and Britain in Asia and then led policy makers to conclude that a strong and liberal America might achieve in Indochina what a weakened and colonialist France had failed to accomplish. In World War II, the United States had sought ties with Southeast Asian nationalists in building an alliance against the imperial forces of Japan. With the defeat of Japan, America turned away from Asian nationalist groups in order to strengthen relations with Britain and France to achieve European recovery. In 1949, the triumph of Mao Tse-Tung's communist forces in China further affected American relations with nationalist movements. This led to the creation of the Southeast Asian Treaty Organization and the search for strategic bases. The loss of China as the 1940s drew to a close had the most profound effect on American policies throughout the 1950s.

With the outbreak of the Korean War, the military imperative of NSC 68 (National Security Council Document 68) came into its own, providing a comprehensive strategy for the containment of the Soviet Union. NSC 68 recommended there be no negotiations with the Soviet Union until the United States had achieved

certain "conditions of strength" necessary to force the dominant
communist power to "change its policies drastically." It favored
the development by America of the hydrogen bomb, the rebuilding
of conventional military forces, a substantial increase in taxation to
meet the costs of military expansion, and the strengthening of a
worldwide anticommunist alliance system. For Asia, it offered a
strategic doctrine around which Americans could unite to win the
Korean War and to assist the French in their struggle in Indochina. The victory of the communists in China, the outbreak of
hostilities in Korea, and the recognition of Ho Chi Minh's government by the Soviet Union and the People's Republic of China
combined to justify the containment by the United States of
monolithic communism. New threats were identified as an outgrowth of communism's worldwide strategy including guerrilla
warfare and subversion. To meet these threats, new American
policies were announced, including liberation, massive retaliation,
and counter-insurgency. The domino theory became a rally cry
calling for the protection of individual Southeast Asian states to
prevent them from falling one by one to communist aggression.
Southeast Asia and Indochina assumed increasing importance for
policy makers not only because of their strategic importance but
because the area as the "rice bowl of Asia" was adjudged essential
to the region and to Japan's continued industrialization.

The first signs of a major shift from the policies of the 1940s and
a movement toward reformulating the national purpose came in
1952 with the election of President Dwight D. Eisenhower and
policy debates in his administration following the defeat of the
French in Indochina. One of President Eisenhower's campaign
promises was that he would end the war in Korea. A Korean
settlement short of military victory which would probably have
been impossible for a Democratic candidate was conceivable for a
popular American general and wartime hero. The momentum
which surrounded the exploitation of anticommunist thinking by
the junior senator from Wisconsin, Joseph McCarthy, was not
strong enough to prevent Ike from seeking a compromise peace in
Korea. Once negotiations were underway, the picture of the enemy
as an implacable and uncompromising foe with whom democratic

states could not do business began to break down. The middle 1950s also witnessed, however, the surrender of the French garrison at Dien Bien Phu in May, 1954, and in this case the American secretary of state appeared to cling to the precepts of NSC 68 and earlier strategic doctrines by refusing to negotiate directly with representatives of the Soviet Union and of the People's Republic of China on such issues as elections in Vietnam or the recognition of Ho Chi Minh.

Thus two opposing views of the means appropriate for coping with issues in the Cold War coexisted for a time in the 1950s. One view which was embraced by President Eisenhower and certain American senators, favored limited contacts and cautious probes through negotiations extending from the working diplomatic level to meetings at the summit. The other views, which in general was defended by Secretary Dulles, transferred the viewpoint of the 1940s to a changing international scene. It proclaimed the dual threat of China and the Soviet Union, the former now surpassing the latter in Asia. Significant rivalry between the two communist states was discounted and the concept of monolithic communism remained undisturbed whether manifested in great power conflicts or guerrilla warfare in Malaya, the Phillippines, or Indochina. A network of treaties was thrown up by America to hold back worldwide communist expansion: ANZUS (Australia and New Zealand) in 1951; South Korea in 1953; SEATO (United Kingdom, France, Australia, New Zealand, Pakistan, the Philippines, and Thailand) in 1954; and Taiwan in 1954. Finally, the rhetoric of Secretary Dulles' policies of rollback, massive retaliation, and liberation carried staunch anticommunist undertones.

President Eisenhower gradually introduced a different strain of thinking into the Cold War; the more inflexible attitudes of the 1940s were slowly pushed into the background. The president became more directly engaged in efforts at arms control leading to the Open Skies proposal in 1955, the Nuclear Test Ban Conference in Geneva, and the Surprise Attack Conference in 1958. At the same time, the president put greater stress on the buildup of conventional military strength supported by low-yield tactical nuclear weapons as a means of implementing policies of flexible re-

sponse. A revised basic national policy statement—NSC 5809—
outlined a wider range of strategic responses including the training of indigenous police forces and the expansion of covert activities. The communist threat came to be seen less as monolithic and
more as many-sided. The Dulles policy which some described as
pactomania (the multiplication of regional security arrangements
against communist aggression around the world) had little effect
in deterring aggression. Nation-states proved unwilling to follow
the dictates of regional security groups when they conflicted with
their interests.

Thus the 1950s, which began as a continuation of the 1940s,
witnessed gradual, often unarticulated and nearly imperceptible
changes. A complex model of the main sources of conflict replaced
the simplified image of monolithic world communism. The Eisenhower administration, whatever its political rhetoric, instituted
policies of accommodation with the Russians and of political and
economic consolidation at home. In the words of a principal author
of NSC 68: "Their view was that the Truman-Acheson policies
had put too great a burden on domestic support. In other words,
the amount of effort being asked of the country in support of the
Marshall Plan, military aid programs, and all the things that had
been cranked up in the Truman-Marshall-Acheson regime asked
too much of the country."[6] The interaction between domestic and
international politics influenced the changing image of international conflict. "Congress was providing less domestic support and
the Korean War was eroding public support. Therefore, one ought
to cut back on involvement abroad and address oneself more to
securing domestic support."[7] President Eisenhower and Senator
Robert Taft at a famous meeting on Morningside Heights at
Columbia University agreed on cutbacks in defense spending of five
billion dollars. Support programs for policies to resist communist
aggression were reduced and programs of retrenchment were pursued, affecting both international and national policies even
though events such as Sputnik led to a return to some of the
policy directions that President Truman and Secretary Acheson
had followed.

What matters most for purposes of this discussion is that the defense of policies became more complex and difficult in the 1950s. The picture of the world struggle as between totally good and evil forces began to change. With the rise of two independent centers of communist power, it became more difficult to point to a single world capital as the source of each successive threat to peace and security. Moreover, the willingness of President Eisenhower to negotiate with communist foes reduced the effectiveness of efforts to portray our rivals as implacable and demonic states.

The 1950s are difficult to assess, in part because the nation's chief executive for eight years remained a leader about whom scholars and political commentators held divergent views. One school of thought pictured General Eisenhower as a reluctant, almost wholly nonpolitical incumbent who chose to stand above the battle and had little zest for partisan struggles. Ike fed and nurtured this viewpoint. As wartime leader, he had defended allied strategy against its critics who charged that Soviet advances in the heart of Europe could have been forestalled by linking the political objectives of the West with its military strategy. He insisted he was a soldier whose responsibility was winning the war while saving American lives; he was not a political or diplomatic leader. Yet in the early 1950s both political parties sent delegations to SHAPE in Paris to enlist him as their candidate for the presidency. His response to their approaches helped reinforce the image of a leader who not only held aloof from party conflicts but justified his approach for reasons of health and personal circumstances. Prominent Americans including Ralph Bunche, social scientists such as Pendleton Herring, and later his faculty colleagues at Columbia University reported that Ike had set well-defined conditions for acceptance of the nomination, including playing golf at least twice a week, reportedly on his physician's orders. From the outset, he was an enigma in the intellectual community, which has its disproportionate share of outspoken interpreters of presidents, and he became an enigma to those who draw up the roster of great American presidents: the historians, the pollsters, and the pundits.

Another school of thought which has only recently appeared, prompted perhaps by nostalgia for the 1950s and the need for reappraisal of Eisenhower as political leader and policy maker, has

gained attention in the 1970s. Political scientists such as Professor
Fred Greenstein of Princeton and popular writers Gary Wills and
Murray Kempton have argued that Ike was a highly political
leader who concealed his political intentions but was acutely mindful of political consequences. Greenstein has had access to new
evidence and sources, especially that contained in several thousand
documents in the Whitman file in the Eisenhower Library. These
documents, made available by Eisenhower's personal secretary,
Ann Whitman, include lists of Ike's appointments, notes, and
·transcripts of informal meetings and conversations, draft speeches,
letters, and a confidential diary. Taken together, they confirm a
quotation that revisionists like to cite from Richard M. Nixon
intending to show that Eisenhower was a more complex and political man than generally appreciated and that "he applied two,
three or four lines of reasoning to a single problem and . . . usually
preferred the indirect approach."[8] He kept a low profile, held to a
crowded schedule including "political" appointments of which
many were "off the record," turned to trusted advisors like his
brother Milton Eisenhower for lengthy consultation, and combined
the use of informal, smaller meetings with top national security
officials and formal ones such as National Security Council meetings. The former were used for policy debate; the latter for consensus building and "spreading the word," that is, educating officials on major policies.

Eisenhower has inspired revisionist political scientists to revisit
his administration. They point particularly to his willingness to
delegate authority. Interest in this aspect of his leadership has been
generated by contrast with the skepticism of some of his successors
toward bureaucracies and bureaucratic politics. After Eisenhower,
with the possible exception of Presidents Johnson and Ford, successive presidents have tended to centralize decision-making power
in the White House. Ike's trust in subordinates was not uncritical.
(For example, he viewed Secretary John Foster Dulles as well-
informed in foreign policy but insensitive to the opinions and
reactions of those he sought to persuade.) He was not beyond using
subordinates to fight in the trenches while he walked the high road
(Dulles was the cold warrior and Ike the peacemaker), and he

fostered the public's illusion that others, for example Sherman Adams, were responsible for what were often unpopular decisions and were the activists whose policies he passively endorsed. Cabinet officials had ready access to the president and were seldom discouraged from arguing their position in cabinet meetings. He reserved freedom of action and safeguarded his reputation for moderation by allowing subordinates to take controversial stands while he stood above the fray. When Press Secretary James Hagerty remarked he would be torn apart by his critics if he defended a controversial position, Ike responded: "My boy, better you than me."[9]

President Eisenhower undertook work politically on two levels. He was untiring in seeking to preserve his standing as a national leader deriving from his historic role as the nation's wartime hero. On another level, he undertook to lead with what Greenstein has called "a hidden hand" as in his behind-the-scenes struggle to diminish the influence of Senator Joseph McCarthy. By never mentioning the senator by name, the president systematically prevented McCarthy from counterattacking and exploiting his conflict with the executive. On sensitive political questions at his press conferences, he deliberately practiced tactics of obfuscation using garbled and fuzzy prose which was in direct contradiction to the care with which he drafted personal correspondence and sharpened and revised the texts of major speeches. His frequent claims at press conferences that he was unfamiliar with the background and details of concrete policy issues are refuted by his notes and minutes of preconference briefings. In his conduct of office and in guidance of subordinates, he was ever mindful that incautious statements by public officials might bring on national and international crises. He wrote with some pride: "By consistently focusing on ideas rather than phrasing, I was able to avoid causing the nation a serious setback through anything I said in many hours over eight years of intensive questioning."[10]

The revisionists have made a persuasive case for President Eisenhower's strengths as a political leader. Such reinterpretation is unquestionably timely and overdue, and by restating the principles underlying the president's approach, they have helped to right the balance. They help us to understand some of the reasons the president was able to draw on the support of broad segments of public opinion without canceling out their enthusiasm by becoming a lightning rod for popular grievances. His care and circumspection particularly in foreign policy helped him to avoid diplomatic errors; he was able to prevent dangerous situations from becoming international calamities. His standing as the commanding general of Allied forces in World War II made him immune from hard-line critics who liked to denounce anyone seeking accommodation and peace. The margins within which the president exercised leadership were greater because of his national and international stature. Because of his personal popularity and his now reasonably well-identified political skills, President Eisenhower left office having preserved the peace and without suffering the precipitous decline in public support his successors were to experience.

If revisionism has helped to right the balance in history's judgment of Dwight D. Eisenhower's presidency, the question remains whether this revisionist school will suffer the fate of revisionism in every other sphere of historical writing. While answers to this question are premature, it is possible now to formulate the questions on which a larger answer must rest. For example, the post-revisionist scholar almost certainly will ask what effect the president's evasiveness had on public understanding. "If the trumpet gives an uncertain sound, who shall prepare himself to the battle" (I Corinthians XIV: 8). The president in a sense operates under what the social psychologists call a double bind. If he says too much, as presidents such as Woodrow Wilson and Jimmy Carter have been wont to do, he provokes opposition. If he says too little and compromises too much, he may leave policy makers and the public without an anchor for their thought.

President Eisenhower was vulnerable to the second of these forces, saying too little, for three reasons: his political style, opposition from the right wing of the Republican party, and the use by his administration, perhaps for the first time, of public relations techniques. The revisionists have given us a full account of the Eisenhower political style, but their critics suggest he paid a high price for the tactics of his approach. On the Eisenhower approach to opposition, Professor Morgenthau has written: "Misunderstanding what 'opposition' means in American political life, the Eisenhower administration continuously and vainly tried to appease its real opposition which is within the Republican party, and it at the same time blessed, if not actively participated in, the attempts of that very opposition to stigmatize as the perpetrators and condoners of treason that very group within Congress and within the country which in terms of numbers and conviction provides the most solid support for the foreign policies the Eisenhower administration would have liked to pursue."[11] Symbolic of what Morgenthau has called the "subversion of foreign policy" was the dependence of the Eisenhower administration for defense of its principal foreign policies on Senator William Knowland, the most outspoken critic of those policies. As the president sought to avoid controversy with the public, he thought in terms of peaceful cooperation with the Congress rather than rivalry as foreordained by the Constitution. As Professor Edward Corwin pointed out, the vagueness of the Constitution on the ultimate responsibility for the conduct of foreign policy is "an invitation to struggle for the privilege of directing foreign policy." Presidents from George Washington to Harry S. Truman accepted this challenge, but President Eisenhower proved willing to surrender to the Congress, particularly on his China policies. Eisenhower never openly challenged the opposition within his own party who gave assurances that the communist regime of China could be overthrown and Chiang Kai-shek's rule restored through the use of air power and naval blockade, using Formosa as a springboard. By appearing to accept the expectations and objectives of the opposition, the Eisenhower administration invited judgment by the standards of its critics alternately apologizing to its allies for accepting such objectives and to the opposition for failure to achieve them. It was responsible enough to avoid military adventures but irresponsible in making bold gestures or well-advertised announcements ("unleashing Chiang Kai-shek") which were not followed up. By allowing itself to become a prisoner to an opposition that clung to an impossible objective, the Eisenhower regime postponed and made impossible a reformulation of American foreign policy and helped bring on the crisis in Vietnam. "President Eisenhower's thinking was dominated by two basic assumptions: that of the two-party system in which the President's party supports the executive branch while the other party opposes it, and the assumption of the equality, in separation, of the executive and legislative branch with regard to the conduct of foreign policy. Both assumptions are completely at odds with the constitutional principles and political practices of the American government . . . [especially with] the political revolution which . . . [had] transformed the American political scene in the last twenty-five years." For: "The general political and social outlook and the specific policies which this revolution has pushed to the fore are supported by a solid majority of the people but not by a majority of the Republican Congress."[12]

To be elected, an Eisenhower or a Nixon had to identify himself with the policies and outlooks of his party, but to govern and conduct foreign policy he had to rely on the main bulk of the Democratic party and at best a tenuous majority of Republicans (half of whom are often in opposition to the changes of the last quarter century). Eisenhower understood the imperatives of foreign policy and the changing forces on the international scene and on the great issues of war and peace pursued a relatively steady course. Yet his inherent conservatism and his misunderstanding of the congressional forces on which he depended for support of his foreign policies led him to miss opportunities to exercise leadership and to educate the public. As a result his administration suffered its severest defeat "on the plane of the imponderables of moral leadership and political prestige."[13] Despite his innate good sense in politics, he yielded to the counsel of Secretary Dulles, who always insisted that Secretary Acheson had suffered defeat because he failed to protect himself on the right flank of the political spectrum. And he failed to articulate the grounds for actions that in themselves were prudent and sound.

One other factor influenced the fate of the Eisenhower administration in the 1950s. The requirements of the mass media came into full force and foreign policy by public relations raised its ugly head. In Professor Morgenthau's words: "It is a peculiarity of the Eisenhower Administration that it is the first democratic government whose relations with the public imitate on a large and institutionalized scale the techniques of public relations experts and commercial advertising."[14] Robert Montgomery, a movie actor, became White House advisor on radio and television. Salesmanship replaced statesmanship. The aim of policy discussion became primarily that of impressing rather than informing the public. Cabinet meetings were televised with heads of departments following their cues. Spectacular announcements were made of five world-shattering shifts in policy which subsequently proved to have almost no relationship to actual policies: liberation, the unleashing of Chiang Kai-shek, agonizing reappraisal, the "new look," and intervention in Indochina.

What Eisenhower began was continued by his successors and the question must be asked whether the gradual decline of public confidence and loss of trust in public statements is not inseparably bound up with this approach to policy. On March 18, 1954, Walter Lippmann, who had supported candidate Eisenhower, characterized the "new look" announced by Secretary Dulles in a speech on January 12, 1954, as "a case of excessive salesmanship" with official explanations of its meaning being so voluminous that "it is almost a career in itself to keep up with them." Similarly, the London *Economist* on August 30, 1952, editorialized: "Unhappily 'liberation' applied to Eastern Europe—and Asia—means either the risk of war or it means nothing." In his State of the Union message of February 2, 1953, President Eisenhower announced he was unleashing Chiang Kai-shek by "issuing instructions that the Seventh Fleet should no longer be employed to shield Communist China." Yet the Eisenhower administration in practice went further than President Truman in limiting Chiang to purely defensive actions.

Thus it remains for future historians to balance the defense or justification of the Eisenhower administration with the judgments of its earlier critics. More serious, the relationship between certain policies and strategies pursued in the 1950s to the events which followed require further and deeper analysis. History follows its own ineluctable course from decade to decade and the seeds of future eras are planted in the past. Strengths and weaknesses in one period are accentuated or reversed in another and societies are condemned to repeat history unless they are more fully apprised of the lessons of the past. Yet from the tangled web, the historian must extract truths though they are elusive and ambiguous.

On no issue is this more true than the effects of certain historical trends and events on shared goals and national purpose. The Eisenhower administration prepared the way for a new era in international relations. In various spheres of foreign policy, the United States moved from confrontation with the Soviets to negotiations. Yet perhaps because of the president's style, the political constraints affecting his policies, and the introduction of a whole new dimension involving public relations, a deep chasm was created between action and exposition. It became increasingly difficult to square policies and pronouncements. Television spectaculars and sloganeering took the place of reasoned explanation. The beginnings of public confusion can be traced to the 1950s, although at the time they were obscured by the enormous residual prestige of a respected national figure. The need for a public philosophy and a clear statement of objectives and policies were recognized (a Commission on National Goals was established) but countervailing forces including "the uncertain sounds" of leadership left the public without direction and guidance.

THE SIXTIES

What was a distant dream in the 1940s became a reality for millions of Americans in the 1960s as the GNP, which passed $200 billion in the 1940s, reached almost $1 trillion by the end of the 1960s. When the economy lagged temporarily, President Kennedy, having promised to get the country moving again, called for an $11 billion tax cut and made heavy outlays for the war in Vietnam and for the race to the moon. Halfway through the 1960s, corporate profits after taxes approached $50 billion. Jobs increased to 78 million and at the close of the decade the median family income was over $8,000. The public purchased up to 9 million automobiles a year.

Yet the public, which beginning in the 1940s had identified the pursuit of happiness with material abundance, remained anxious, dispirited, and discontented. One cause was the gap between the ordinary American and the very rich. Less than 1 percent of the population, or approximately 200,000 families, had annual incomes of more than $100,000. The top one-fifth of all families owned 80 percent of all private wealth. About 15,000 families had net assets of $500,000 or more. Those families whose incomes had increased felt deprived in comparison with the very wealthy and dissatisfied with the results of their own relative affluence. White-collar Americans became increasingly other-directed and they sought satisfaction in a highly visible social life. Lower-middle-class Americans lived on the fringe of the better suburbs. Blue-collar workers found life on the assembly line monotonous and lived in continuous fear of unemployment. Ethnic Americans living in marginal urban areas had a sense of intense competition with black Americans. About 30 million Americans still remained at or near the poverty level.[15]

Whether particular American families had benefited or not from the nation's economic growth, they were as a whole troubled and uneasy, incapable of drawing security or satisfaction from an affluent age. The symbol of this dissatisfaction was the more privileged suburban population. The families who composed this group moved up the ladder exchanging one home for another more spacious and ostentatious. With each ostensible advance, however, the gain to those who measured social and economic status by material possessions proved illusory. To parents and children alike, climbing the social ladder became less a sign of personal well-being than of conspicuous consumption. The material gains and improved standards of living did not bring the new utopia the philosophers of the 1940s had promised, in part because of inflation and in part because of unsatisfied human needs. Social climbing in the 1960s became a treadmill for individuals and material progress left unfulfilled social and psychological hopes and aspirations.

If the national climate was a troubled scene, the international arena had its own residue of doubt and uncertainty. A young and attractive president moved onto the stage with confidence and élan, saying in his inaugural address, "Ask not what your country

can do for you but what you can do for your country." More than
any American president in the electronic age, John F. Kennedy
took hold of the new instrumentalities of the mass media to project his image at home and abroad. Moving presidential press conferences from the old Indian Treaty Room to the State Department
Auditorium, he appeared on a larger and more impressive stage.
The whole world had a chance to see and hear the vigorous young
president. Whereas Eisenhower had been cautious and often evasive in what he chose to say, Kennedy answered questions freely,
seemingly off the top of his head. The role of a full-time White
House press corps was diminished as the wire services drew their
news from the president's live press conferences. The response
around the world and the subsequent sorrow and grief of ordinary
people at the tragic assassination showed how effectively he had
communicated his personality and ideals to people around the
world.

With all his strengths and those of a mighty nation, the president
was called on to counter the effects of two disastrous events. The
Bay of Pigs invasion of Cuba in the first day of his administration
revealed the United States as weak and ineffectual within its own
sphere of influence. Moreover, Kennedy's first meeting with Premier Khrushchev in Vienna was for him a traumatic event as the
Soviet leader tested and threatened his resolve. A chain of events
led from Vienna to Vietnam, reflected in the president's determination to demonstrate that America was indeed strong. His first action
was to send 15,000 military advisors to Vietnam. Thereafter the
Kennedy-Johnson policy in Vietnam moved incrementally toward
the ultimate involvement of 500,000 American troops. Vietnam
became a test case both for America's strength at turning back wars
of national liberation and of a young president's resolve. Policy
makers focused on the development of the capacity to fight limited
wars, proceeding from what proved a valid assumption that most
conflicts in the postwar world would be of a limited character only
indirectly involving both superpowers. The Cuban missile crisis
and the crisis in Berlin were exceptions that witnessed direct con-
frontations between the superpowers.

In Southeast Asia, the Kennedy administration sought to assist the South Vietnamese in building a model democracy while at the same time deterring the possibility of a wider and total war. It introduced new strategies for counter-insurgency and "flexible response" in national security policy. It tended to dismiss the concept of monolithic world communism, tempered the rhetoric of the Cold War, and displayed greater concern for the Third World than any previous administration. Yet despite the president's desire to seek a relaxation of tensions with the Soviet Union, the struggle in Vietnam led to conflicts manifested in other sectors of American foreign policy. If the myth of communist unity was weakened, the doctrine of falling dominoes persisted as a guide to policy that was less expressed but nonetheless was followed. Communist China was seen as the primary instigator of conflict in Northeast Asia and the greatest threat in Southeast Asia. The United States held to policies of containing communism as a single threat even while recognizing the division between China and the Soviet Union.

The major issue in the 1960s regarding foreign policy was not the failure of the national leadership to communicate the basis of American policies, especially in the early years of the 1960s. The problem was rather that liberal and enlightened leaders overestimated America's ability to stay the course and put its stamp on the rest of the world. Kennedy's early promise to come to the defense of freedom everywhere was linked with the debacle in Vietnam. The rather arrogant belief of certain administration figures that the new administration could overturn the Diem regime by cooperating, tacitly at least, with the coup by the generals weakened any prospect of an effective national government in the 1960s. "The best and the brightest" in the 1960s clung to noble ideals and liberal doctrines which despite their appeal had the effect of drawing America ever deeper into an overall defense of freedom in Southeast Asia which constituted an over extension of American power.

The tragedy of the 1960s was less in the realm of thought and perception, however, than in the ability to translate thought into action. Kennedy in particular understood that the simple bipolar world of the 1950s was passing. In his American University speech and other important presidential statements, the president showed he was able to deal with complexity. Failure and disillusionment came later from policies that were followed presenting the American people with an ever-expanding set of commitments in Vietnam: more troops, more aid, more casualties, more failed predictions of "ending the war by Christmas." Added to this, a great debate ensued over guns versus butter. With rising inflation, a devalued dollar, greater competition from Japan and the Common Market, and hesitation to increase taxes, a critical economic situation worsened as the military conflict deteriorated. The issue was not, as liberal policy makers argued, whether history might have taken another turn. The "might have beens" in the implementing of Vietnam policy were numerous. The consequences of "what was" dissolved what had been a firm national consensus to continue the war. President Johnson decided not to run and his loyal and courageous vice president, Hubert Humphrey, was defeated, in part because of the nation's reaction to Vietnam. With all the noteworthy achievements of the 1960s in civil rights, great power agreements on armaments and outer space, significant educational advances and innovation and the sense of movement in society, the shadow of Vietnam hung over the decade. It divided families, turned youth against established institutions, and left a residue of confusion and division. Thus a decade which began as a reversal of a period of consolidation and stasis ended with the nation seeking to regain and recover its lost unity. For some, the 1960s had been a decade of "too much movement," too many youthful leaders, too much pointless violence and senseless bloodshed, and too many new and costly ideas. So the decade led naturally to the 1970s which, as with the 1950s, began as a decade of withdrawal, recovery, and regrouping.

THE SEVENTIES

According to the cyclical view of American history, the 1970s were destined to be an era of consolidation and retrenchment. It seemed that the time had come once again for a pause, for taking stock and for reappraisal. The nation had grown weary of vast social upheavals that had shaken society to its roots. In the aftermath of the civil rights revolution, of near civil war in cities like Newark and Detroit, of three political assassinations, and of conflicts over building a good society at home and a more secure international order abroad with the United States cast in the role of world policeman, Americans responded to urgings that they do less, not more, to change the world.

The change was expressed both in political tactics and campaigning and in the policies of the first Nixon administration. In the election of 1972, the victorious candidate made his main appeal to the silent majority, a body of Americans resentful at being passed over in the 1960s by a government deeply concerned with depressed minorities. Not the Republicans but the Democratic candidate, Senator George McGovern, introduced the slogan "come home America" to describe a scaling down of objectives in foreign policy. President Nixon's domestic affairs advisor, Daniel Patrick Moynihan, coined his own pungent phrase, "benign neglect," to announce a change in the administration's timetable for the problems of minorities and the cities. Rebellious groups would stew in their own juice, lowering the intensity of social conflict.

Much of the impetus toward a lowering of sights in foreign policy stemmed from growing pressures to end the war. In February, 1970, President Nixon announced what reporters at first named the Guam Doctrine, promising that "our interests, our foreign policy objectives, our strategies and our defense budgets are being brought into balance—with each other and with our overall national priorities."[16] The doctrine received a full exposition in the president's foreign policy message to Congress in February, 1971. Nixon, like Eisenhower in the 1950s, sensed that burgeoning defense budgets and worldwide entanglements were eroding public support for government. The nation's economic well-being was jeopardized by the high costs of the Vietnam War. Its relations with friendly states in Europe were endangered by what Europeans perceived as an overcommitment to a military engagement which had grown incrementally and from which their great power ally seemed unable or unwilling to disentangle itself. The Nixon Doctrine was less a well-crafted state paper, such as the Monroe Doctrine, than a general response to a public mood. Its critics pointed out that it represented a commitment to the same level of potential involvement with smaller conventional forces.

However, the Nixon Doctrine resulted from the more limited freedom of action of an administration with less moral and political authority than Eisenhower commanded in the 1950s. As a widely respected military hero, Ike had been able to announce in the 1952 campaign that he would go to Korea to end the war. Not only did President Nixon lack the popularity and prestige to take such a step but the objective circumstances in Vietnam scarcely resembled those in Korea. The military front had been stabilized in Korea and a rough equilibrium of forces established between North and South Korea. In Vietnam, the lines of conflict were in a state of continuous flux. The Korean War was of relatively short duration, whereas Vietnam had been at the heart of American foreign policy since 1965 and a contentious issue since 1954.

Thus the Nixon Doctrine was formulated to demonstrate that never again would the United States be drawn into an international conflict beyond its power to resolve. At the same time it lay the foundations in Vietnam for a gradual ending of hostilities there. It testified to the narrow limits within which American foreign policies could be effective. The authors of one study stated: "Its central thesis is that the United States will participate in the defense and development of allies and friends, but that America cannot—and will not—conceive All the plans, design All the programs, execute All the decisions, and undertake All the defense of the free nations of the world. We will help where it makes a real difference and is considered in our interest."[17]

The Nixon Doctrine expressed a strategy designed to prevent future Vietnams in American foreign policy. On Vietnam and the specific American involvement there, the Nixon-Kissinger approach was based on a series of improvisations to bring the conflict to an end. These included a Vietnamization strategy, military actions in Cambodia, the gradual withdrawal of American troops, appeals to the Soviet Union and the People's Republic of China, and diplomatic negotiations with a North Vietnamese delegation in Paris. Secret diplomacy replaced public diplomacy, reflecting the personal style of both Kissinger and Nixon. The gulf was narrowed between the various sides in the conflict—North Vietnam, South Vietnam, and the United States. The diplomatic skills of the negotiators (Kissinger and Le Duc Tho) won them a joint Nobel Prize, but for South Vietnam and America the effort was too little and too late. It was too little to turn back the tide of the revolutionary movement in North Vietnam which enabled them, despite their shattering losses in men and property and a massive commitment of troops and material by the Americans, "to keep coming." It was too late because intervention by Congress and popular dissatisfaction with a war that went on and on nullified the diplomatic initiatives in Paris, Moscow, and Peking as well as the struggle on the ground.

The last stage of the Vietnam conflict symbolizes the American dilemma in an era in which society's problems have grown more complex and leaders must act within social and political limits. The commitment to national goals in the 1940s appeared limitless. The "we" who defended those goals were freedom-loving people everywhere. The "they" were freedom's enemies, the inheritors of Marxism-Leninism throughout the world. The national consensus that was achieved in the 1940s and early 1950s was founded upon a rather simple picture of the two spheres in the world, of the "we" and the "they," of "democracy" and "communism."

The beginnings of a change occurred in the 1950s as President Eisenhower sought to reduce international tensions and limit the spiraling arms race. International diplomacy is a practical art and its goals are more difficult to articulate than war aims, whether those in a hot war or a cold war. Americans in particular have been schooled to think in politics of victories and defeats, not of truces and settlements and doing the least possible damage to the human race, which some moral theorists see as man's highest end. At another level of human experience, while some of us as experienced parents find truth in the axiom that being a good father means doing the least possible harm to one's children, who among us has not dreamed of guiding and directing them to heights we have been unable to reach? We want our children and our nation to stand above the adversities and limitations that we take for granted in our individual lives. What is beyond us individually, we project into the life of children and the nation. We are driven to making concessions and compromises in personal life, including those inherent in the limitations of our own nature, yet we expect our leaders to do for the nation what none of us can do for ourselves. This is the reason that the public grows impatient with leaders who talk of constraints. It is the reason such leaders speak privately of the limits of national power but in public of national hegemony and universal values.

In the 1950s, the United States and the Soviet Union undertook to ease international tensions through meetings at the summit. In the mid-1950s, the nonaligned nations of the world banded together to strengthen common interests which they chose to identify neither with democracy nor communism. The struggle for freedom on a global basis which a young American president proclaimed in the 1960s collided with the dynamic force of Asian nationalism. And the most outspoken anticommunist twentieth century American president set about achieving a normalization of relations not only with Soviet Russia but with Communist China as well.

Building a popular constituency for the ambiguous requirements undergirding such policies has exceeded the political skills of successive postwar American presidents. Complex social and political tasks require complex explanations. The ingrained clichés of the early Cold War are insufficient to explain political settlements such as recognition of territorial boundaries at the heart of Europe, arms agreements, or the need to create a new balance of power in Southeast Asia which exploits Sino-Soviet or Sino-Vietnamese differences. The struggle that went on in the late 1960s and early 1970s within the People's Republic of China between three contending groups is instructive: the army under Lin Piao, the revolutionaries, and Madame Mao; and the followers of Chou En-lai. The first two contended that the Soviet Union in the north and the Americans in the south were coequal threats to China's security. As long as the war in Vietnam continued, Mao Tse-Tung, who mediated between the three groups, was unwilling or unable to join Chou En-lai in identifying the Soviet Union as the principal threat. Only as the war in Vietnam wound down did Mao accept Chou's argument, identify Russia as the enemy, and move toward normalization and relaxation of tensions with the United States. If American diplomats had understood the struggle in China through contacts which existed in Warsaw and Asia and had tried to explain it, it is difficult to believe that the American people, already divided on continuing the war in Vietnam, would not have turned on their leaders.

Therefore, an American president faced with the task of rallying the public to deal with complexity in foreign policy has three alternatives, none of which is satisfactory. He can speak in broad generalities and hope that, as was true in the 1940s, there is some correspondence between the general statements and the requirements of national interest. Or he can be evasive, hoping by his silence or vagueness to buy time to resolve problems through private actions behind the scenes, as was the approach in the 1950s. Or he can seek to build a reputation for decisiveness as President Kennedy sought to do in Vietnam and the Cuban missile crisis following the Bay of Pigs and his traumatic meeting with Premier Khrushchev in Vienna in the hope that a show of present strength will give room for diplomatic flexibility later.

The diplomatic history of the 1970s hardly encouraged optimism that any past approach or the recent tactics of three presidents in that decade provide answers to the challenge of building support for complex foreign policies. President Nixon sought to bring the war in Vietnam to an end without destroying American credibility as a defender of independent states around the world even though he understood that the United States was overextended; the stakes were too great to withdraw all troops immediately. While gradually withdrawing American troops, he increased bombing activities in the north and mined Haiphong harbor hoping to persuade Hanoi that a political settlement was in its interest. If these actions helped reduce the intransigence of the North Vietnamese, they apparently did little to reassure the Congress, which beginning in the late 1960s and dramatically in the 1970s moved to assert its authority in foreign policy. As long as the conflict in Vietnam was viewed as an outright struggle between irreconcilable social and ideological systems, popular and congressional support was maintained. When the nature of that struggle became more complex and am-

biguous and when the president's course of leadership, inevitably
or not, became more subtle if not devious, congressional support
waned. Bill Moyers is correct when he writes: "Our system assumes
a sense of participation by the people in the making of critical
national decisions. When that sense of involvement is absent, when
the public feels excluded from the judgments that are made in its
name, a policy is doomed from inception, no matter how theoreti-
cally valid it is."[18]

Foreign policy, however, may also involve the balancing of
seemingly opposing objectives and here Moyers' formula becomes
more difficult to apply. Indeed the most recent president in the
1970s, Jimmy Carter, would appear to have run afoul of precisely
the opposite problem for which his predecessors in the late 1960s
and early 1970s were condemned. Candidate Carter in language
reminiscent of Woodrow Wilson promised to conduct an open foreign policy. He campaigned against the secret diplomacy of Secretary Henry Kissinger and his walk down Pennsylvania Avenue following the inaugural address was intended to symbolize trust in the
people. President Carter's openness soon created problems in forging a consistent foreign policy, for in speaking out freely on
sensitive diplomatic issues at presidential press conferences, he
often spoke off the cuff in language that he and subordinates had
to reformulate when diplomatic shock resulted. His recourse to a
form of diplomacy that commentators characterized as media
diplomacy left allies bewildered and the public confused. Because
he chose to speak out so freely, he created the impression of ama-
teurism and naïveté and his policies appeared inconsistent even
when the broad directions were reasonably consistent. By contrast
the successes in Carter's foreign policy—the Panama Canal Treaty,
the Camp David agreement, and the trade agreement negotiated by
Robert Strauss have all been based on patient, quiet diplomacy
whose results are open to the public but whose long tedious processes are not grist for the media, in part because of their complexity.

The 1970s were a decade in which pessimism set in over the
nation's capacity to resolve complex national as well as international problems. Contradictory as it may seem, the self-doubt of nation-

al leaders skeptical that solutions can be found to complex problems has been accompanied in the seventies by a profusion of bold
new plans to save society by special interests and minority or
single-purpose groups. The corollary of the decline in national
consensus from the decade of the 1940s to the present is the rise
of fragmentary groupings who have discovered for themselves a
common purpose which they are unable or unwilling to recognize
in ideas of public interest and the general good. Man will not
tolerate a vacuum. When religion disappears, some form of nationalism or secular faith takes its place and when consensus on
the nation's goals declines, subnational groups come forward with
their own peculiar faiths. In the late 1960s, youths turned against
the faith of their fathers not because its precepts were faulty but
because in the eyes of youth they were not being observed. It will
be a long time before historians sift out the wheat from the chaff,
the good from the bad in the "youth revolution." With all its
naïveté and moral pretentiousness, it may contain lessons for the
future about excessive materialism (although here one detects a
note of hypocrisy), the environment, abuse of power, diets if not
drugs, truth in government and business, equal opportunity,
broken families, loneliness, and mutual respect and caring. The
tragedy of the youth revolution was the absence of genuine dialogue. The late sixties and early seventies were a time for straight
talk, but instead Americans over forty sulked in their tents quar-
reling endlessly over haircuts or rock music while others curried
favor by imitation and blind adulation for youth. If youth were
the first special-interest group who confused the public interest
with their own values and self-centered goals, they at least embraced a broader vision, however inchoate and ill-defined, of what
they proposed as good for society as a whole. And those who now
serve in government and business have demonstrated an ability of
adapting some of their goals to practical reality.

It would be difficult to say the same for all the single-interest
groups which have followed: Proposition 13, pro- and anti-abortion
groups, opponents of gun control, narrowly based ethnic groups,
so-called religious cults, backlash political and religious movements,
segregationists, segments of various liberation and anti-liberation

groups, and lobbies for narrowly based economic gains, all zealously and relentlessly pressing forward to gouge the public. Spokesmen for each group appear to be saying: vote for our cause and we will remain citizens of the Republic; oppose us and we will turn against all the orderly processes of society, government, and business. Worse still, they unhesitatingly move beyond their areas of competence and concern to become self-appointed diplomatic envoys, authorities on economic growth, and outspoken political critics and advisors to the president. With the decline of political parties in the selection of political candidates, they hold the balance of power in tightly contested elections of congressmen and senators, perhaps even of presidents.

The nation has had interest groups before, but in the 1970s, their place in American society has changed in three important respects: they have proliferated in numbers, they have narrowed their focus, and they have come to play a more decisive role in the political process. In place of spokesmen for the cities as a whole, we have political delegations sent to Washington to bail out a particular city. Instead of representatives of business and industry, it is the rescue mission for Chrysler which confronts public officials. Yet curiously, the rhetoric of those who seek help is one of condemnation of the very public agencies to whom they turn for survival and thus further erodes the public trust and the national consensus. These groups cannot see the irony that they press their narrow claims in an interdependent system with general problems so bewilderingly complex that even the most broadly based and coherent views are unlikely to be sufficient.

The 1970s, therefore, have been years in which the complexity of both national and international problems has increased along with growing doubts and fears that solutions could not be found; they have also been years of political and economic fragmentation (on the international scene, American diplomats must do business with the representatives of 150 countries varying greatly in size, values, and interests). To complete the equation, culturally and psychologically another profound change has occurred. A personal example may serve to illustrate the change. When I joined the staff of a large private foundation in the mid-1950s, its trustees were men of broad and comprehensive vision. They had been chosen to serve not because of specialized knowledge and interests but because they were preeminently generalists and renaissance men: Raymond Fosdick, Henry Alan Moe (president of the Guggenheim Foundation), Robert Lovett, Lewis Douglas, Ralph Bunche, Arthur Houghton, Jack Kimberly, Lee DuBridge, Robert Goheen, Theodore Hesburgh, and others. Sometime in the 1960s and extending into the 1970s, a change took place and the underlying reasons for the change are more important than personalities. It was argued that the Fosdicks, the Moes, and the Lovetts had been admirable trustees but their interests belonged to a bygone age. The new challenges in the 1960s and 1970s called for dramatic responses to urgent, unprecedented problems. The foundation had to seek trustees who were capable of evaluating these problems as participants and of finding as activists relevant solutions. To this end, the chairman of the board and the president set out in search of blacks, youth, and women, labor leaders, environmentalists, agronomists, and demographers. Only specialists were capable of guiding the foundation; generalists had become passé.

What happened in miniature in my little corner of the foundation world was occurring in government, business, and education (it became the first criterion for a college or university president that he be a problem solver or an expert in conflict resolution). Diplomats for the new age, we were told, must be economists, military men, businessmen, or area studies men because of the specialized content of the new diplomacy. The time span for answers to urgent problems had been shortened telescopically and civilization could not wait for the slower-working intellectual processes of the generalist. One consequence was the change in the composition of decision-making bodies. From once having been assemblies of wise men, they became bodies in which each trustee and each official became a defender of his own special interest, whether minorities or the media or military strategy, whether the environment or food production or population control. For a foundation president or an ambassador who in turn had been chosen for his or her specialized competence to give this proliferation of particular interests a unified focus and coherence was a task which approached

that of Hercules' holding up the world. Yet this was the burden
that the 1970s placed on its leaders at almost every level of society.

It is possible that the tasks of the 1970s and the complex inter-
relationship of persistent problems exceed the grasp of any mortal
man or group of men. A former secretary of state has remarked,
"Today's problems make pygmies of us all." We are ingrates in
condemning "the best and the brightest" of our leaders for failing
to resolve issues to which we have found no answers. It may well
be that government has become unmanageable and its problems
insoluble as we move into the 1980s. The best men can do may
indeed be to look for small-sized answers to fragments of large-
scale problems.

Yet it seems unlikely that civilization will settle for this, particularly in large nation-states governed as what Paul Appleby
liked to call "big democracies." The lessons of the 1970s, however
much they may cut across the grain, may be that society and its
leaders will have to continue to look for more coherent approaches
and better ways of coping with complex problems—which they
then must be prepared to explain to themselves and to the world.
No comment is more frequently heard when an American travels
abroad than: "We are confused by your nation's leadership." In
part such confusion is inevitable: America is a great sprawling
country spanning a continent and its people speak with many
voices. Throughout its history, its differences have given it a vitality which early observers like Bryce and de Tocqueville could not
find in equal measure in any other nation. The uncertainty and
doubts about our present condition must reflect something else,
however; they relate to what we are today and what we appear to
be, the national consensus or lack thereof, the steadiness of our
course and the condition of "e pluribus unum." In the absence of
a public philosophy, it seems unlikely we can radiate conviction on
great national purposes. If our policies seem more designed for
domestic politics and "show-business," we will probably not im-
press old and new friends in other lands. The rediscovery of common values and the moral foundations of democracy may be something about which we can do very little until the tides of history
come in once again.

One thing we must do, however, is to focus on government at the highest level and reflect on the presidency, its tasks and its tendencies, its sources of strength and conditions of weakness. A group of business leaders recently met with the nation's chief executive for discussions of the energy problem. They were impressed with the president's technical mastery of the subject; he had drawn together a prodigious mass of complex data reminiscent of the breathtaking command of details candidates have demonstrated in recent presidential debates. As the business leaders left the Oval Office, one particularly wise man turned to a companion and asked "What would his presentation have been like if he had left the details to his technicians and given us the benefit of a broad vision of where society should be heading and where we must fall back, what sacrifices must be made, how competing groups can be encouraged, even coerced to adjust their claims, and what government can and can't do in helping us all realize such a vision." Because our problems are so complex, there is an urgent need for minds that see them whole. Because special interests have proliferated, the demand grows apace for someone to identify points of convergence. Because values are in flux, the challenge of restating common goals and purposes must take priority. Because the public philosophy has been weakened, leaders must look for ways to renew it. Since politics and diplomacy have their ambiguous dimension, requiring both private give and take and public debate, someone must make this clear on the political hustings no less than in presidential papers. Finally, because national power is not unlimited, the nation in domestic and foreign policy must neither shrink from its responsibilities nor commit itself beyond its powers. In Reinhold Niebuhr's words: "Nations as individuals, may be assailed by contradictory temptations. They may be tempted to flee the responsibilities of their power or refuse to develop their potentialities. But they may also refuse to recognize the limits of their possibilities and seek greater power than is given to mortals."[19] Our capacity to use our power creatively but avoid both sloth and pride may in fact be enhanced by the fact that we are no longer all-powerful.

11

The Open Question:
The Future as Challenge
and Response

America's future is bound up with the future of the presidency, and the future of Western civilization with America's future. To make such a statement is to recognize the distribution of forces in the world, not to yield to chauvinism or national self-righteousness. Despite the alarms periodically sounded by militarists that the United States has lost its strategic superiority and by liberals that American culture has decayed from within, the Republic remains one of the two mightiest world powers and the presidency potentially the most powerful executive office of any representative government.

At the same time, more than at any point in its history the nation is imperiled by dangers from within and outside its borders. Its survival and that of civilization is endangered by the prospect of thermonuclear destruction; its unity is in jeopardy because of the fracturing of the American system of governance. The unraveling of the social fabric is being spurred by the breakdown of private and public trust. Old problems persist and new dilemmas perplex national leaders. A once buoyant and exuberantly self-confident national mood has been supplanted by a brooding sense of anxiety and fear. The American who radiated optimism and hope only a few short decades ago has been overwhelmed by a sense of his own limits, impotence, and hopelessness. For the public, the cycles of progress and retrenchment that have marked the nation's adaptation to change in past generations no longer relieve inner tensions. Powerful new instruments of communications and information widely advertised as a transforming source of mass

education and public understanding have complicated and confused the pursuit of the public interest. Political reforms that promised improved and more democratic governance have weakened
the presidency, shattered the mediating role of political parties,
divided the Congress, confounded executive-legislative relationships, diminished the stature of political leaders, and increased the
possibility of political deadlocks. Troubled leaders acknowledge
that their most cherished "solutions" to the nation's urgent problems have failed or are no longer relevant. The society's health is
endangered, paradoxically, by both scarcity and abundance: too
many people with too great an abundance of resources and too
many specialized advisors. They suffer as a result from too many
unfulfilled aspirations thwarted by too many unrewarding forms
of employment and too many unsolved problems generating ever
higher levels of frustration and disappointment. Americans who
struggled with the perils of affluence in the 1950s and 1960s had by
the mid-1970s confronted both abundance and scarcity with no
overall solution in sight.

In the midst of its burgeoning problems, the nation's trauma
and confusion has intensified with the loss of the historic anchors
of its political and cultural faith. Not only have ancient institutions such as the church, the family, and the state been weakened
but a once vital public philosophy has lost its hold on millions of
Americans. Private gain has crowded out the public interest as
society's foremost guide and standard. Because aggressive special-
interest lobbies and single-interest groups have made their voices
heard, the remaining spokesmen for the common good are crowded
out from the center of political discourse. Those leaders of thought
and opinion who have traditionally occupied a middle ground
calling for a long view of the nation's problems have lost out to
those who oversimplify, promise painless answers, and are unwilling or unable to engage in political analysis and moral reasoning.

It would be wrong to attribute the nation's problems to a lowering of the country's intelligence. More people enjoy the advantage
of improved education than ever before in the nation's history,
even though the gap persists between the well-educated and the

poorly educated segments of the population. We have better birth
rates, death rates, tax rates, growth rates, and emigration rates and
better statistics on inflation, divorces, unmarried couples, personal
income, and consumption patterns. While raw knowledge is greater,
the factors to be assessed and interrelated have increased exponentially to a bewildering degree. Instead of isolated issues and
rivalries, problems proliferate around the habitable globe. Their
solution has become so painful and the weight of contingencies so
overwhelming that for the wisest statesman policy making is at
least three-fourths guesswork.

One response to present perplexities is to turn for leadership
to the technicians. An engineering approach reassures those who
have abandoned all hope of mastering the last detail but gain
confidence from leaders who for every problem quote columns of
statistics and hard data. However, recent history teaches that
social engineering has had its chance with planners and social and
economic technicians who have failed to bring social progress,
domestic tranquillity, or international peace. Moreover, not only
have policies crafted by high-powered technicians failed but the
public has grown dispirited and disillusioned in the absence of a
framework of political thought which would give meaning to
techniques and strategies. If present trends continue, society may
bury itself in an avalanche of hard and soft data without ever
being enabled to comprehend the purposes for which data and
strategies must be applied.

No one would deny that in the present crisis diagnosis is easier
than prescription. It is not enough to call for a public philosophy
and assume that what is necessary is possible. To invoke the example of the Federalist Papers is a beginning but hardly a sufficient
answer. As a beginning it is a turning away from prevailing present-day political perspectives and a return to an ancient tradition
of moral and political reasoning. The problems to be addressed are
as different in scale and magnitude as America as superpower is
different from the fledging Republic. A society that would throw
off the shackles of preoccupation with mechanics to rediscover
political truths and moral values must combine, as Alfred North
Whitehead prescribed, reverence for its enduring symbols with

freedom to revise those symbols. For a nation to cut itself adrift from its political traditions is to float aimlessly and without purpose in an ever larger alien sea. For a government whose approach is not anchored in some enduring body of political thought, inconsistent and contradictory policies become inevitable. For the public, comprehension of the course its leaders are following is blurred by policies and actions following one another without any apparent relationship to one another or to any established set of controlling ideas and principles.

A public philosophy cannot offer a blueprint for every conceivable action or policy. It is less a guidebook than a way of thinking about politics. It can help both leaders and the public to view separate political actions in a wider context. For a mighty nation anxious about its present and future, it can strengthen hope and resolve by establishing links with its past thought and experience. In this sense, a public philosophy can be a window opening on an uncertain future.

THE OPEN QUESTION: WHITHER AMERICA?

The open question for Americans for the 1980s and beyond is how and whether "a nation so conceived and so dedicated can long endure." That Lincoln should have posed this question in the midst of a great civil war was not surprising. Yet when leaders raise the issue today, the public tends to divide among those who praise and those who condemn prophets expressing concern. Society is disposed either to recognize and honor those who look ahead or denounce them as doomsday philosophers who spread defeatism and gloom. Yet surely America's leaders in its third century have a responsibility to anticipate the future. Although historians speak of an empire's "thousand year reign," the life span of most civilizations and states seldom exceeds three or four hundred years. If it is an open question whether the United States can survive as the world's supreme leader, angry voices from the right or left should not go unanswered when they seek to close off discussions of the future. It may be "good politics" for extremists to challenge a president or a secretary of state when he warns that the future of the Republic is in question, but whether or not it is good politics to shout down reasonable men who express concern, it is bad history. It is also an expression of blind chauvinism and political "machismo-ism" more fitting for a street fighter than for a responsible public servant.

Looking ahead, then, is an important dimension of political leadership and of any emerging public philosophy. In an era when America had a public philosophy it aspired to share with the world, successive leaders worked to construct their own coherent philosophies of politics and history. Like the scientist who cannot rule out the possibility of rampant disease or epidemics going unchecked, the founding fathers recognized that a public philosophy had to leave room for both sickness and health, weakness and strength. If incurable pessimists are unlikely to be the architects of a viable public philosophy, neither are positive thinkers and political boosters from whom optimism is more a tactic to promote themselves than to strengthen the nation. Society must be on guard against both the doom-sayers and the super-patriots, for as Alexander Hamilton wrote: "I never expect to see a perfect work from imperfect man. The result of the deliberations of all collective bodies must necessarily be a compound . . . of the errors and prejudices . . . the good sense and wisdom, of the individuals of whom they are composed. . . . How can perfection spring from such materials?" (*The Federalist*, No. 85).

If the Constitution has endured, it is in part because of the classic exposition of the public philosophy undergirding it which Hamilton laid out in *The Federalist*. If the Constitution has become "the venerable patriarch" of the world's written public charters, its long life must in part derive from its linkage with the public philosophy. The fact that this philosophy was wrought in crisis and controversy is an object lesson for the future. The great documents of statecraft almost never are produced in ivory towers or issue from the establishment's fifty-fifth floor offices. Instead they have been forged in the heat of battle generated by bitter political conflicts. Not only *The Federalist*, but the Declaration of Independence, the Emancipation Proclamation, and the Four Freedoms were born in crisis when the nation's independence and survival hung in the balance. The great declarations of public philosophy were timeless statements of the nation's goals formulated when the nation was in jeopardy.

In much the same way that individuals resist talking about their own mortality in ordinary times, national leaders who seek popular acclaim boast of their country's hegemony in the world, not the possibility of its decline. The war of words then becomes a contest between a sense of history and the imperative of politics with politics assuming its least noble form in selfish partisanship. Inquiry concerning the nation's future is sacrificed on the altar of shortrun politics. Worst of all, those who would address "the open question" are pilloried and condemned.

IMPLEMENTING AMERICA'S FUTURE

When the lessons of past civilizations are spread out before us, and America's future approached as an open question, the question remains: How is any leader to follow the course the historian has charted? How can a nation realize the goals and implement the policies necessary to meet the challenges of the future? Historians and theologians, speaking from the heights, call on men to make moral responses. Statesmen, including presidents, must descend into the valley of moral and political dilemmas. Pontiffs may affirm sacred values; politicians must look for the effects of any single value carried to its logical conclusion. The latter must heed the counsel that no moral end in politics should be pursued divorced from its probable consequences or in disregard of its connections with other moral ends. The theologian who prescribes is often like a man from a far country who ventures onto strange soil and proceeds to teach before he has learned what is troubling a people. No one can invalidate moral and religious teachings. The mischief is done when moral teachings have immoral consequences, as with "holy wars" that produce mass murder, evangelism that leads to personal self-righteousness, or holiness which generates human conflict and cruelty. The statesman must remember Cromwell's appeals to the representatives of the Church of Scotland: "I beseech you, in the bowels of Christ to think it possible you may be wrong."

The historian and theologian rightly point to the connection between religion and democracy, yet that connection is more complex and subtle than fanatics and moralists understand it to be. Americans in a secular age may have drifted too far from "the Higher Law" tradition of the American constitution. The ultimate justification of democracy is moral because it is the one political system that seeks in a comprehensive way to institutionalize human dignity—politically and spiritually as well as materially and socially. If discipline and efficiency are the only criteria, including efficiency in promoting and realizing a single moral end, then an authoritarian order, whether secular or sacerdotal, is equal to or better than democracy. It is not surprising that spiritual leaders who speak out of a background of authoritarian traditions are impatient with the conflicts that moral and political differences generate in a democracy. They search for fixed laws and rules to put an end to disputes and confusion.

Religion's most powerful teaching is the law of love, but love is not easily translated into politics. Love calls for self-denial and self-sacrifice. Within the family, love is capable of transforming anxious striving and bitter rivalries into mutual respect and selfless sharing of everyday burdens and blessings. Within the family, love is never as fully understood as when a family experiences its absence. When unremitting family strife replaces mutual respect, human personality risks self-destruction. Love is the reunion of the separated, yet separation and estrangement have become the driving force in much of society, including the family. In the last two decades of the twentieth century, generation has turned against generation, social and ethnic groups are pitted against each other, and struggling organized religions promote disunity. Moreover, love as the law of life is in tension with the attainment of certain values. If men love one another to the point of judging every man's values as equal to all others, how can a family or a civilization judge structures as good and evil, better or worse? If rigid moral structures are maintained by too much coercion, individualism and human vitality are endangered. Far more than is often realized, there is an inevitable tension likely to persist until the end of time between loving and respecting the unique individual and building hierarchies of moral values.

The president in his leadership inescapably contends with all the stubborn contradictions of modern life. If he possesses a sense of history, he is more likely to respond creatively to the perplexing challenges on which the future depends. Yet, however wise and understanding, he is trapped by the necessities of choice and the impossibility of providing an ever more diverse public with a satisfying account of his actions. He is caught between cynics who call on him to be hard-boiled and moralists who demand he do what is right as they see the right. Where his predecessors had recourse to silence and restraint, he must stand before the judgment of the mass media as would a defendant pleading his own case to jurors in adversary proceedings. Perhaps never in human history have the burdens of public office been greater. Never has the road of political leadership been so treacherous or the hazards of false turns so painful. For as he moves across perilous terrain, the political leader must be cautious yet courageous, moral yet practical, inspiring yet effective, consistent yet experimental, and in tune with both domestic and international politics.

A president, it is argued, must provide a moral example and instruct the people. To the extent he succeeds in this task, he must mediate between moral principles and political realities. His guide in foreign policy must be the national interest. To the degree he ennunciates high moral truths, they must be filtered through the screen of what he conceives to be good for the nation. Pope John Paul II could say in his address to the United Nations on October 2, 1979, that wars will be prevented, not by arms but by moving beyond the symptoms of war to its causes—hunger, poverty, and inequality. A president must know that his oath of office requires that he provide for his nation's security in a world where war and the test of arms remains the final arbiter. For the pontiff, "Everything will depend on whether . . . differences and contrasts in the . . . possession of goods will be systematically reduced . . . on whether the belts of hunger, malnutrition, underdevelopment, disease and illiteracy will disappear from the economic map of the world." A president must rally a reluctant public that feels itself hard-pressed and deprived and must persuade unbelievers of the need to give help to others in greater need while simultaneously strengthening the nation's economy so that its own citizenry may be served. His Holiness as moral leader can press Catholic doctrine on divorce, contraception, and abortion—three profoundly divisive issues in American society—while saying: "I hope that the state authorities . . . will enjoy the confidence of all for the common good."[1] The president as political leader of all the people must seek reconciliation of the moral issues that divide the nation. If the president is a moral leader, he must perform that role as honest broker, hoping in Lincoln's words that history will bring him out all right. In 1890, Woodrow Wilson in an address at the University of Tennessee spoke of "the leaders of men," declaring: "Those only are the leaders of men who lead in action. . . . The men who act stand nearer to the mass than the men who write. And it is in their hands that new thought gets its translation into the crude language of deeds."

If America and its leaders are judged by "the crude language of deeds," an observer who gives the nation its due can discern streaks of grey in the night. If the nation were entering the twilight of its existence, would rich and poor alike in the international community turn to it for leadership? Would the world's spiritual leaders be accorded freedom to speak out to a troubled people hour after hour on the mass media? Would the majority of citizens anxious about providing energy and shelter for themselves and threatened by spiraling inflation continue to favor help to the world's underprivileged? Would the nation's critics at home and abroad cherish the belief that they remain free to criticize and known that Americans would continue to listen responsively to criticism?

Furthermore, the nation and its leaders can point to achievements in precisely those areas that historians identify as primary causes of a civilization's decline. Civil rights leaders who warn of complacency about equal opportunity for minorities also acknowledge that never in history has a forgotten group advanced as far as American blacks in the 1960s and 1970s. Not by accident, Pope John Paul II visiting the United States in 1979 found that American women, having moved ahead dramatically in the last decade, were raising their voices more strongly on the question of ordination of women than women anywhere else in the world. However troubled is the state of the American family, children and young adults have found outlets within the family for self-expression and moral independence that young people are struggling to attain in other lands.

Politically, not only is the Constitution intact as the oldest written charter of government but peaceful political succession has been preserved without debate or question. Despite all the clamor about government being unmanageable, participants and civil servants are mobilized on an unprecedented scale from every sector of society: business and labor, youth and the aged, and religious and secular leaders. The political process remains a system of checks and balances with the executive, legislative, and judicial branches each playing their roles as vigorously as at any time in American history. Political devolution is not only proclaimed but practiced throughout the federal system with grants-in-aid and block allocations in programs which run the gamut from the arts to youth. Voluntarism, which de Tocqueville described as uniquely American, while weakened in some sectors, is alive and well not only in many local communities but nationally in the work of Common Cause and in consumer and environmental reform movements such as Ralph Nader's. The dread problem of class warfare that has undermined and destroyed other societies has been held in check by the relatively favorable opportunities for blue-collar workers moving up the ladder.

In regards to international relations, the United Nations forum has its home in the largest American city. An American president has provided worldwide leadership in focusing attention on human rights. The United States, while seeking to maintain a strong national defense, has since the days of the Baruch proposals on atomic controls provided continuing leadership in successive disarmament debates. Nor should we forget that it was the American president who had been the country's most respected general as commander of the Allied Forces in World War II who warned the public of the military-industrial complex. Of how many countries could it be said that informed and outspoken critics of the nation's participation in an unpopular conflict, such as the Vietnam War,

could speak to attentive and open-minded listeners at the nerve
center of military planning, the nation's war colleges? Militarism
in the conduct of war has consistently been held in check by
civilian leadership in the Defense Department. Anticolonialism
after World War II was voiced more strongly by Americans than
by the leaders of any other industrial state.

And religion, whatever the debates over the relationship between church and state, has continued to provide a model of religious liberty for people everywhere. Not surprisingly, the author
of the statement on religious liberty at Vatican II was an American, Father John Courtney Murray. Though ecumenism has waxed
and waned, its stronghold has been the churches of America. An
American Catholic became the thirty-fifth president of the United
States despite predictions this would never happen.

The nation survived a presidential resignation, three tragic
assassinations, and the decision of another president not to seek
reelection because of an unpopular war. And in the late 1970s, an
American president felt able to go before a national television
audience acknowledging his failures and asking the people to support him in a new attack on the nation's gravest problems, energy
and inflation. If courage to admit mistakes and go on with renewed
determination are a sign of national health, America must be seen
as yet responding to its severest challenges. There is good reason,
therefore, and considerable evidence to support the historian's
judgment that America's future is an open question. Whatever the
alarms that may be sounded, the determined efforts of free men
suggest that trend is not destiny, that new challenges remain both
dangers and opportunities, and that a society with as much resili-
ence may have its best days ahead of it.

The presidency gives America a platform for renewing and restating in the days ahead the public philosophy. The elements of
such a philosophy can be found not only in tradition but also in
measured responses to present problems. Moral reasoning can be
the medium in which such a philosophy is hammered out. The
task should be within the means and resources of a good and decent
people. No enterprise is more deserving of the efforts of the president and the public.

Notes

INTRODUCTION

1. Samuel H. Beer, "In Search of a New Public Philosophy," in Anthony King (ed.), *The New American Political System* (Washington: American Enterprise Institute for Public Policy Research, 1978), 5.
2. *Ibid.*, 6.
3. *Ibid.*, 44.
4. Everett C. Hughes, "Professions," *Daedalus*, XCII (1963), 656, 657.

CHAPTER 1

1. James S. Young, "The Troubled Presidency: II," New York *Times*, December 7, 1978, Op-Ed page.
2. Meg Greenfield, "It Really Isn't So Complicated," *Newsweek*, January 15, 1979, p. 96.

CHAPTER 2

1. Reinhold Niebuhr, *Beyond Tragedy: Essays on the Christian Interpretation of History* (New York: Charles Scribner's Sons, 1955), 113.
2. *Ibid.*, 118.
3. St. Augustine, *The City of God* (New York: Modern Library, 1950), Bk. XIX, Ch. 4; Bk. V, Ch. 19.
4. Herbert Deane, *The Political and Social Ideas of St. Augustine* (New York: Columbia University Press, 1963), 62.
5. St. Augustine, *City of God*, Bk. XIX, Ch. 11.
6. Niebuhr, *Beyond Tragedy*, 121.
7. *Ibid.*, 122.
8. *Ibid.*, 124.
9. Niccolò Machiavelli, *The Prince and The Discourses* (New York: Modern Library, 1940), 63–64.
10. Harold Nicolson, *Diplomacy* (London: Oxford University Press, 1939), 43–44, 50.
11. Niebuhr, *Beyond Tragedy*, 125, 126.
12. *Ibid.*, 130.

13. *Ibid.*, 131.

14. *Ibid.*, 132.

15. Winston S. Churchill, *The Gathering Storm* (Boston: Houghton Mifflin, 1949), 320–21, 207–209. Vol. I of *The Second World War.*

CHAPTER 3

1. Arnold J. Toynbee, *Civilization on Trial* (New York: Oxford University Press, 1934), 25.

2. Quincy Wright, *A Study of War* (Chicago: University of Chicago Press, 1942), I, 198.

3. Jacob Burckhardt, *Force and Freedom* (New York: Pantheon Books, 1943), 134–35.

4. Edward Gibbon, *The Decline and Fall of the Roman Empire* (New York: Modern Library, 1932), 93–95.

5. Lewis S. Soloman, *Multinational Corporations and the Emerging World Order* (Port Washington, N.Y.: Kennikat Press, 1978), 10. Peter J. Buckley and Mark Casson, *The Future of the Multinational Enterprise* (London: Macmillian, 1976), 12.

6. Fred Bergsten, Thomas Horst, and Theodore H. Moran, *American Multinationals and American Interests* (Washington, D.C.: Brookings, 1978), 7–8.

7. Letter to the author from Ambassador Soedjatmoko dated August 7, 1979.

8. Hans J. Morgenthau, *Politics Among Nations: The Struggle for Power and Peace* (5th ed.; New York: Alfred A. Knopf, 1978), 6–7.

9. *Ibid.*, 7.

10. Leopold S. Amery, *The Washington Loan Agreements* (London: Macdonald and Company, 1946), 154.

11. Charles Kindleberger, *Power and Money: The Economics of International Politics and the Politics of International Economics* (New York: Basic Books, 1970), 21–22.

CHAPTER 4

1. Walter Lippmann, *Early Writings* (New York: Liveright, 1970), ix.

2. James Fallows, "The Passionless Presidency," *Atlantic Monthly*, May 1979, p. 42.

3. Ross J. S. Hoffman and Paul Levack (eds.), *Burke's Politics: Selected Writings and Speeches of Edmund Burke* (New York: Knopf, 1949), 106.

4. Sander Vanocur, Washington *Post*, October 31, 1976.

5. Paul Nitze, "Eight Presidents and Their Different Approaches to National Security Policymaking," in Kenneth W. Thompson (ed.), *The Virginia Papers on the Presidency* (Washington, D.C.: University Press of America, 1979), 54.

6. Thomas E. Cronin, *The State of the Presidency* (Boston: Little Brown, 1975), 118–19.

7. James S. Young, "The Troubled Presidency," New York *Times*, October 6, 1978, Op-Ed page.

8. *Ibid.*

9. Walter Lippmann, *The Public Philosophy* (New York: New American Library, 1955), 137.

10. John Roche, "The Founding Fathers: A Reform Caucus in Action," *American Political Science Review*, LV (December, 1969), 815–16.

11. Richard Hofstadter, *The American Political Tradition and the Men Who Made It* (New York: Knopf, 1948), 16.

12. Alex de Tocqueville, *Democracy in America* (New York: Vintage Books, 1945), II, 140–41.

13. Henry Steele Commager (ed.), *The Living Thoughts of Thomas Jefferson* (Greenwich, Conn.: Fawcett, 1963), 88; George Washington, "Farewell Address," in Henry Steele Commager (ed.), *Documents of American History* (New York: Appleton-Century-Crofts, 1949), 173.

14. Hans J. Morgenthau, *Politics Among Nations* (5th ed.; New York: Alfred A. Knopf, 1973), 40.

15. Ralph Ketcham (ed.), *The Political Thought of Benjamin Franklin* (Indianapolis: Bobbs Merrill, 1965), 345.

16. John Adams, *Discourses on Davila* (New York: De Capo Press, 1973), 27.

17. Dean Rusk. Letter to the author, January 24, 1979.

18. Thucydides, *The Peloponnesian War* (Ann Arbor: University of Michigan Press, 1959), 126.

CHAPTER 5

1. Dumas Malone, *Jefferson and His Time* (Boston: Little, Brown, 1948), I, 227.

2. *Ibid.*, 226.

3. Alexis de Tocqueville, *Democracy in America* (New York: Vintage Books, 1954), II, 144.

4. *Ibid.*

5. *Ibid.*, 145, 146, 147.

6. Robert J. Lifton, *History and Human Survival* (New York: Random House, 1970), 325.

7. Rollo May, *Man's Search for Himself* (New York: W. W. Norton, 1953), 216.

8. Philip S. Foner (ed.), *Basic Writings of Thomas Jefferson* (Garden City, N.Y.: Halcyon House, 1944), xiii.

9. Paul Findley, *Abraham Lincoln: The Crucible of Congress* (New York: Crown, 1979).

10. Quoted in Herbert Butterfield, *The Peace Tactics of Napoleon, 1806–1808* (Cambridge University Press, 1929), 48.

11. Meg Greenfield, "That Crazy Statistical Feeling," Washington *Post*, September 5, 1979, A17.

12. George Washington, Letter for Transmittal in Convention, September 17, 1787, in *The Federalist* (New York: Modern Library, 1937), Appendix IV, 586.

13. Alexander Hamilton, James Madison, John Jay, *Federalist Papers* (New York: New American Library, 1961), 322, 320.
14. *Ibid.*, 197, 91, 226.
15. David Hume, *Essays*, I, quoted *ibid.*, 574.

CHAPTER 6
1. Abraham Lincoln to Horace Greeley, August 22, 1862, in T. Harry Williams (ed.), *Abraham Lincoln: Selected Speeches, Messages, and Letters* (New York: Holt, Rinehart and Winston, 1957), 191.
2. Jean-Francois Revel, *TheTotalitarian Temptation* (New York: Penguin Books, 1976), 41–42.
3. Alexander Solzhenitsyn, *Lenin in Zurich* (New York: Bantam Books, 1977), 32.

CHAPTER 7
1. Roanoke *Times*, August 2, 1979, p. 5.
2. Theodore M. Hesburgh, *The Hesburgh Papers* (Kansas City, Andrews and McMeel, 1979), 121.
3. *Ibid.*, 121, 120.
4. Paul A. Freund, *On Law and Justice* (Cambridge, Mass.: Harvard University Press, 1968), 8.
5. Hesburgh, *The Hesburgh Papers*, 134.

CHAPTER 9
1. Telford Taylor, *Munich: The Price of Peace* (Garden City, N.Y.: Doubleday, 1979).
2. Harold Nicolson, *Diplomacy* (London: Oxford University Press, 1939), 11.
3. *Ibid.*, 11–12.
4. General Sir John Hackett and Other Top-ranking NATO Generals and Advisors, *The Third World War: August 1985* (New York: Macmillan, 1978), 49.
5. *Ibid.*
6. *Ibid.*, 51.
7. Kenneth W. Thompson (ed.), *The Virginia Papers on the Presidency* (Washington: University Press of America, 1979), 17.
8. Hackett, *The Third World War*, 275.

CHAPTER 10
1. Theodore H. White, *In Search of History* (New York: Harper and Row, 1978), 308.
2. Arthur Schlesinger, in Lloyd C. Gardner *et al.*, *The Origins of the Cold War* (Waltham, Mass.: Ginn and Co., 1970), 43.
3. Herbert Feis, *From Trust to Terror: The Onset of the Cold War, 1945-50* (New York:W. W. Norton and Company, 1970), ix.
4. Joseph Schumpeter, *Capitalism, Socialism, and Democracy* (New York

and London: Harper and Brothers, 1947), 51.

5. Joseph Schumpeter, *Business Cycles* (New York and London: McGraw Hill Book Company, 1939), I, 405n.

6. Paul H. Nitze, "Eight Presidents and Their Different Approaches to National Security Policymaking," in Kenneth W. Thompson (ed.), *The Virginia Papers on the Presidency* (Washington, D.C.: University Press of America, 1979), 37–38.

7. *Ibid.*

8. Richard Nixon, *Six Crises* (New York: Doubleday, 1962), 161.

9. Gordon Hoxie (ed.), *The White House: Organization and Operations* (New York: Center for the Study of the Presidency, 1971), 4.

10. Dwight D. Eisenhower, *Mandate for Change, 1953–1956* (Garden City, N.Y.: Doubleday, 1963), 478.

11. Hans J. Morgenthau, *Politics in the Twentieth Century* (Chicago: University of Chicago Press, 1962), 422. Vol. I of *The Decline of Democratic Politics.*

12. *Ibid.*

13. *Ibid.,* 424.

14. *Ibid.,* 413.

15. Norman A. Graebner, *The Age of Global Power: The United States Since 1939* (New York and Toronto: 1979), 151.

16. Richard M. Nixon, "U.S. Foreign Policy for the 1970s," in *A New Strategy for Peace* (Washington: Government Printing Office, 1970).

17. Richard G. Head and Ervin J. Rokke (eds.), *American Defense Policy* (3rd ed.; Baltimore: Johns Hopkins University Press, 1973), 75–76.

18. Bill Moyers, "One Thing We Learned," *Foreign Affairs,* July 1968, p. 657.

19. Reinhold Niebuhr, *The Irony of American History* (New York: Scribner's, 1962), 130.

CHAPTER 11

1. Pope John Paul II, New York *Times,* October 3, 1979, p. B 5.

DATE DUE